Genealogy of Mazo, Curry, Thompson, Mason, Forsythe, Brown, Shatteen, Washington, Morgan, Robinson, Alston, Frazier, Hapton et al

Thompson Family History v. 7 of Nassau, Bahamas; Chatham, Jefferson & Washington Counties, GA; and Allendale, Barnwell & Beaufort Counties, SC

MARC D. THOMPSON

Family histories require constant revision. As this century moves along, more and more information becomes digitally or electronically disposable. Older information may be discarded or destroyed. If we do not save this information, it may be lost forever. Please contact author with any corrections or additions. marc@VirtuFit.net.

ISBN: 978-0-9883440-7-5

Photography by Marc D. Thompson

MARC D. THOMPSON, VIRTUFIT.NET™

www.VirtuFit.net • marc@VirtuFit.net

Skype: VirtuFit

ideafit: www.ideafit.com/profile/marc-d-thompson

Also by Author

Other Books by the Author:

Fitness Book of Lists © 2012

Poems...Of Eternal Moments © 2012

Genealogy Of Romano, O'Connor, McCabe, Morrison, Carmona, Smith, Barrett, Kilmartin, Vitale, Quintavalle, Reilly, McLean, Brown, Boles, Nocton, DiSimone, Viviano, DiStefano, Cutumachio, Tully, Kirrane, McGowan, et al © 2012

Thompson Family History © 2005

This book is dedicated to

Melvalean Curry Thompson, 1967-2008

Foreword

Why do people seek to learn about their family history? Years ago, Marc asked me for information about our relatives. He was eager to start the journey into the past. As of today, I believe Marc has answered the question. He wanted to view our lives more fully. Marc enjoys solving the multitude of mysteries regarding family histories and it is revealed in his family history volumes.

While visiting Marc, he asked me to visit a local library to search for information regarding a family's ancestor. Fortunately, I found the information Marc needed. Suddenly, I realized how searching for long ago addresses, pictures, and families is a wonderful way to reflect back to how and why things happened; in a way, making sense of it all! Marc truly knows how to present the past to each of us as we look toward the future. Allow his thirty years of research skill and efforts take you on a journey around the world!

Shirley M. Duncan

Preface

Our 30 years journey of knowledge has led to a plethora of information. We have learned much. We have discovered our roots, good and bad. It has molded us. We have found we are related to some famous and infamous folks and there are some areas of the country that are named for our distant families.

We are direct-line descendants of King Philip of France and the Royal families Cleves. We are descended from Civil War servicemen Elijah Anderson, Thomas E. Batdorf, Andrew G. Hensel, Daniel Updegrove, John H. Wert, Louis L. Stewart and Jacob Wittle, War of 1812 servicemen Adam Frantz and Andrew Hensel, and Revolutionary War servicemen William Anderson, John Daniel Angst, Philip Jacob Bordner, Peter Brown (British), John Faber, Casper Hensel, John George Herrold, Jacob Lehman, Michael Leymon, Andrew Messerschmidt, John Miller, John Balthaser Romberger, Jonas Rudy, John George Schupp, John Peter Shaffer, John George Felten and Gottleib Zink. Our ties also include European Mayors John Guerne and John Emmerich, religious leaders John Peter Batdorf, John Batdorf, John George Bager Jr., John George Bager Sr., John Heilferich Lotz , George Gaukel and Entrepreneur Alexander Thompson.

We are direct-line descendants of the some famous homesteads and locations, including the George Bager Homestead, Abbottstown, PA, the Chris Miller Homestead, North Lebanon Township, PA, the George Mennig (Minnich) Homestead, PA,the Thomas Benfield homestead, Berks Co., PA, the Livesey Homestead, Philadelphia, PA, and the Wirth Homestead, Lykens Valley Golf Course, Dauphin Co., PA (demolished

1989). Additionally, our ancestor's names were immortalized at these locations: Bordnersville, Kelly crossroads, Livesey Street, Herrold's Island, Keefer's Station, Deibler's Gap, Deibler's Dam, Shoemakertown, all in Pennsylvania. Finally, our ancestors had surnames named after the Jura Mountains of Switzerland and Acri, Italy, among other locations.

We are collateral descendants of Presidents Dwight D. Eisenhower and William McKinley and Pennsylvania politicians Samuel Pennypacker, John Morton and Jonas Row. Civil War Brigadier General Galushia Pennypacker, Entertainers Marlon Brando, Les Brown and Ray W Brown, Religious leaders Conrad Weiser and Michael Enderline, Melba Dodge, Jesse Runkle, Enrico Caruso and Galla Curci are all cousins. Lastly, Taylor Wittel lists relations to James Madison, Zachary Taylor, Jefferson Davis and Gene Autry. This volume will serve to honor us with the researched and documented information of our background.

Our ancestry was derived from this data, the Thompson Family History (TFH) genealogy, which includes:

7,460	Relatives in TFH
2,063	Marriages in TFH
1,292	Places in TFH
1,167	Sources (over 5,000 Sources not producing information) for TFH
1,113	Surnames in TFH
361	Media in TFH
20	Generations (12 Generations in format) in TFH
95	Age of oldest ancestor at death, Sarah E Wirt & Mrs. M. Curcio
89	Ancestors named John or Albert
85	Ancestors named same male name, John, Johannes, Jean, etc
82	Ancestors names Sophia (4) or Maria (78)
74	Ancestors named same female name, Mary, Maria, Mary Ann, etc.
51	Ancestors named Dolores or Ann
50	Most variations for single surname, Batdorf, Bodorff, Buderff, Pottorf,

38	Ancestors named Mary or Frances
34	Ancestors named Shirley or Mary
27	Number of letters of longest female ancestor's name, Amelia Dorothy
24	Number of letters of longest male ancestor's name, Howard Andrew
22	Age of youngest ancestor at death, Andrew Morton & Henry Rudin
21	Ancestors named Connor (1) or Adam (20)
17	Ancestors named Andrew (16) or Roman (1)
16	Youngest age when first child born, Myrtle A. Thompson & Fortune
13	Ancestors named Mary Ann
11	Number of countries ancestors born in, DEU, ITA, IRL, SCO, ENG, FIN,
7	Most different ancestral lines with same surname, Miller, Mueller, etc.
6	Number of states ancestors born in, PA, NY, DE, GA, SC, VA
5	Ancestors named Tyler (1) or Anthony (4)
5	Ancestors named Tiffany (1) or Rachel (4)
4	Ancestors named Paul or Paolo
4	Ancestors named Ed or Edward
3	Ancestors who died at sea, N. Benesch, G. Rieth & G. Shoemaker
2	Ancestors named Ashley (1) or Renae (1)
1	Ancestors named Gerald or Gilbert
49%	Relatives born in Pennsylvania
19%	Relatives born in Germany
16%	Relatives born in Scotland
9%	Relatives born in Italy
5%	Relatives born in Georgia
5%	Relatives born in South Carolina
5%	Relatives born in Ireland
2%	Relatives born in New York
1%	Relatives born in Switzerland
<1%	Relatives born in Virginia, Florida & West Indies

Acknowledgments

Thanks to my parents without whom I wouldn't exist, and hence their parents, ad infinitum. Thanks to my sisters, for being there for me and showing interest in our history. Thanks to Joe who tutored me as a teen at the Pennsylvania State Library Genealogy room. Thanks to my hundreds of cousins, close and distant, that selflessly donated their hard–worked family histories to me. Thanks to every clerk and registrar, cemetery manager and LDS employee, who gave their time to help me discover our roots. This book is truly the love of thousands.

Table Of Contents

Introduction ·· 1

Chapter One ··· 5

    Pedigree ·· 6

    Family History ·· 7

Chapter Two ·· 59

    Photos ··· 60

    Photos ··· 61

Chapter Three ·· 63

    Places ·· 64

Chapter Four ·· 83

    Kinship ·· 84

Chapter Five ·· 105

    Calendar ··· 106

    Possible Data Errors ·· 118

Afterword ··· 123

    Bibliography ·· 125

About the Author ··· 171

Index ·· 173

Introduction

Genealogy was created for people to know the history of their lineage; to discover their origins; to prove bloodlines and royalty. Responding to their deep desire to understand and discover their past, this volume was compiled. It shall stand as part of the legacy of their ancestry.

Our mission is to document and record all that is available for our direct line and reap the enjoyment that this discovery brings. The first goal of the Thompson Family History (TFH) was to amass photographs of as many ancestors as possible. As a face can tell a thousand tales, so much can be learned from them. The second goal of the TFH was to document the medical background of our ancestors, so our children can lead a healthier life. The third goal of the TFH is to amass documentation of our ancestors in order to extend the lineage and to lead to information about the personality (biography) of our forefathers. Our ancestors are not a mere name. They have tales to tell, journeys to documents. They have accomplishments and setbacks. They have memories worth telling. They have goals, glories, and personalities. The Irish Kings would orally pass down their regal history. They would recite a list of names, their kin, noting outstanding events associated with the forbearers. The ancient Scottish bards similarly memorized their royal family, reciting the pedigrees of the Old Scot's Kings, regardless of the complexity.

Genealogy is a duty. The day we bear children, we took the responsibility of passing along our history. We are responsible for the knowledge of their grandparents and all the wisdom that comes with this knowledge. Our duty, then, includes our children's heritage, the names and faces of their forefathers and mothers. The medical history and genetic backgrounds of their blood lines; the Princes and the paupers; the photographs and historical areas and properties; the tragedies and joys. This TFH is our heritage and with this information we can be proud of ourselves, our past and aim toward a bright future and better lives. If our duty is neglected, as each generation passes, so will our family history.

Most genealogies tend to trace a descendancy or the paternal line (single ascendancy). Our purpose was to trace all ancestors with equal perseverance. This is a monumental, if not impossible, task. We have compiled a pedigree, beginning with our children and using an ahnentafel format. Our children are generation 1, their parents are generation 2, their grandparents are generation 3, etc. There is a family group sheet for each pair of parents along the pedigree. The emphasis at present is on generations 1 through 10, although we have researched as far back as generation 20. Additional collateral ancestors have begun to be added as of 2005. In most cases, the Anglicized first and middle names were used throughout the TFH. For example, Johann Heinrich is John Henry and Orsala Francesca is Ursula Frances. The most commonly found surname was used, whether Anglicized or not. The majority of the collateral information was derived from the US census records. To preserve privacy, information on living persons has been removed or privatized.

As genealogists will agree, no family history is 100% accurate. We have made errors as others have before us. As this century moves along, more and more information becomes digitally or electronically disposable. If we do not save this information, it may be lost forever. The TFH is a guide for future generations who may use this information for their own goals, whatever it maybe. We have given our children a foundation. Take it, improve it, embrace it. The continued excellence of this genealogy will be improved by the following plan.

A. Correct errors and complete Source Citations.

B. Collect photographs and medical history of ancestors.

D. Document more personal information of ancestors leading to increased biographical information.

E. Expound on current family group sheets and extend parentage.

F. Begin the written biographical volumes (narratives)

I have a desire and I have a bond. I have a desire to know from whence we came. I want to know our history, our origins. I want to know what our ancestors did, how they persevered and how the spark of life made it way from Geoffrey Livesay born 1410 in England to Sophia born 2004 in Florida. I feel a bond. I have a strong connection to the late 19th century.

If I were given the opportunity to live in any era, I most certainly would pick the 1860-1880's. The time was simple and the people were honest. People worked hard and took pride in their family, their home and their reputation. When I look into the eyes of our ancestors from this time period, I feel a link. I would have fit nicely in their time. Read and enjoy.   Marc D. Thompson

Chapter One

Our family's pedigree and history.

Our ancestors and their family history, plus the details of the life and times of all of our relatives, including the cited sources.

Pedigree

Edward "Ned" Mason

b: 1847 in Washington Co, GA
m: Abt. 1869 in Washington Co, GA
d: Bet. 1888–1900 in Washington Co?, GA

Mack Mason

b: September 25, 1880 in Washington Co, GA
m: December 15, 1902 in Washington Co, GA
d: September 18, 1962 in Daughter Annie's Home, Savannah, Chatham Co, GA

Ranie Brown

b: December 1852 in Washington Co, GA
d: Bet. 1910–1920 in Washington Co?, GA

Ned "Eddie" Mazo

b: September 07, 1912 in Jefferson Co, GA
d: December 20, 1997 in Sumter Regional Hospital, Americus, Sumter Co, GA

Peter Thompson

b: February 1860 in Jefferson Co, GA
m: May 19, 1881 in Washington Co, GA
d: Bet. 1900–1910 in GA?

Sarah "Sallie" A Shalteen Thompson

b: June 1883 in Washington Co, GA
d: March 21, 1938 in Augusta Rd., Chatham Co, GA

Anne Shatteen

b: Abt. 1865 in Washington Co, GA
d: Bet. 1884–1900 in GA?

Melvalean Curry

b: January 15, 1967 in Jefferson, Philadelphia Co, PA
m: November 21, 2001 in Media, Delaware Co, PA
d: May 29, 2008 in Delray Beach, Palm Beach Co., FL

Percy Campbell Forsythe

b: January 1882 in Bahamas, West Indies (Eng)
m: Abt. 1923 in GA?
d: January 19, 1942 in Chatham Co, GA

Robert J Washington Forsythe

b: September 15, 1925 in Savannah, Chatham Co, GA
m: April 17, 1948 in Savannah, Chatham Co, GA
d: November 22, 1999 in Seattle, King Co, WA

Nina Washington

b: October 31, 1908 in Daufuskie, Beaufort Co, SC
d: August 05, 1944 in Charity Hospital, Savannah, Chatham Co, GA

Delores Ann Curry

b: February 24, 1948 in Savannah, Chatham Co, GA
d: December 16, 2000 in Chestnut Hill Philadelphia, PA

Frederick "Freddie" Curry

b: February 22, 1907 in Savannah, Chatham Co, GA
m: September 17, 1928 in Savannah, Chatham Co, GA
d: November 13, 1964 in Savannah, Chatham Co, GA

Lucretia "Cressie" Jo Curry

b: March 05, 1929 in Savannah, Chatham Co, GA
d: December 10, 1998 in Liberty Regional Medical Center, Hinesville, Liberty Co, GA

Elizabeth Brown

b: Bet. 06–June 11, 1911 in Allendale, Barnwell (Allendale), SC
d: October 16, 1965 in Chatham Co, GA

Family History

Generation 1

1. **Melvalean Curry**, daughter of Ned "Eddie" Mazo and Delores Ann Curry was born on January 15, 1967 in Jefferson, Philadelphia Co, PA. She died on May 29, 2008 in Delray Beach, Palm Beach Co., FL. She married **Living Thompson** on November 21, 2001 in Media, Delaware Co, PA, son of Living Thompson and Living Duncan. . .

    Notes for Melvalean Curry:
    Mel was named after her great uncle "Melvin" and her mother's maiden name Dolores "Curry." Curry is possibly from the Old English name Maethelwine which meant "counsel friend". Curry is the Anglicized form of Gaelic Ó Comhraidhe, descendant of Comhraidhe, a personal name of uncertain meaning. [author, 2006]

    Notes for Living Thompson:
    Marc was named after "Mark" Twain and from his mother's maiden name, Shirley "Duncan" Marc Duncan Thompson derived from "Ares Strong-willed son of Twin"

    Mark is the familiar form of Marcus, a Roman praenomen, or given name, which was probably derived from the name of the Roman god Mars. Saint Mark was the author of the second Gospel in the New Testament. He is the patron saint of Venice, where he is supposedly buried. Another famous bearer of this name was Mark Antony (Marcus Antonius), the Roman triumvir who was the lover of Cleopatra. Duncan derives from the nickname from Middle Low German dunker 'dark' Duncan from Dankert, German, meaning 'strog-willed.' Thompson derived from 'son of Thomas, the twin.' [author, 1989]

Generation 2

2. **Ned "Eddie" Mazo**, son of Mack Mason and Sarah "Sallie" A Shalteen Thompson was born on September 07, 1912 in Jefferson Co, GA. He died on December 20, 1997 in Sumter Regional Hospital, Americus, Sumter Co, GA[1, 2]. He met **Delores Ann Curry**.

3. **Delores Ann Curry**, daughter of Robert J Washington Forsythe and Lucretia "Cressie" Jo Curry was born on February 24, 1948 in Savannah, Chatham Co, GA[3, 4]. She died on December 16, 2000 in Chestnut Hill, Philadelphia, PA.

    More About Ned "Eddie" Mazo:
    b: September 07, 1912 in Savannah, Chatham Co, GA[5]
    Census: 1920 in Atlanta, Fulton, GA[6]
    Census: 1930 in Birmingham, Jefferson, AL[7]
    Residence: 1930 in 2231 5th Ave., Birmingham, AL
    Census: 1940 in Atlanta, Fulton, GA[8]
    Occupation: Cook[9]
    Education: Grammar School[10]
    Military Service: Bet. November 23, 1945-April 18, 1947 in Air Corps, MOH (Hawaii)[9, 10, 11]
    Social Security Number: 253-16-1557[1, 2]
    Residence: 1997 in Plains, Sumter, GA[2]
    Residence: 1997 in 225 Hospital Drive, Plains, Sumter, GA[2]
    Funeral:[1]
    Occupation: Small Machine Operator (Construction)[2]
    Burial: December 23, 1997 in Anderson Nat'l Cemetery, Andersonville, Macon, GA[2, 12]
    Cause Of Death: Cause of death was deleted from Death record[5]

    Notes for Ned "Eddie" Mazo:
    Ned "Eddie" Mazo was named after grandfather Ned Mason and from a military acquaintance named Mazo [author, 2003]

    Born 01-01-1916 Bibb Co, GA [Certificate of Death, #054861, Sumter, GA, State Registrar, Atlanta, GA]

    More About Delores Ann Curry:
    Religion: 11 Mountz St., Savannah, Chatham Co, GA[13]
    Occupation: Homemaker
    Burial: December 20, 2000 in Green Mount Cemetery, Philadelphia, Philadelphia Co, PA
    Medical Condition: asthma

More About Ned "Eddie" Mazo and Delores Ann Curry:
Other-Begin:

Delores Ann Curry and Ned "Eddie" Mazo had the following children:

1.   i.   Melvalean Curry (daughter of Ned "Eddie" Mazo and Delores Ann Curry) was born on January 15, 1967 in Jefferson, Philadelphia Co, PA. She died on May 29, 2008 in Delray Beach, Palm Beach Co., FL. She married Living Thompson on November 21, 2001 in Media, Delaware Co, PA, son of Living Thompson and Living Duncan. . .

      ii.   Living Mazo (son of Ned "Eddie" Mazo and Delores Ann Curry).

Generation 3

4.   **Mack Mason**, son of Edward "Ned" Mason and Ranie Brown was born on September 25, 1880 in Washington Co, GA[14]. He died on September 18, 1962 in Daughter Annie's Home, Savannah, Chatham Co, GA[15, 16, 17]. He married **Sarah "Sallie" A Shalteen Thompson** on December 15, 1902 in Washington Co, GA[18, 19, 20].

5.   **Sarah "Sallie" A Shalteen Thompson**, daughter of Peter Thompson and Anne Shatteen was born in June 1883 in Washington Co, GA[18, 19, 21]. She died on March 21, 1938 in Augusta Rd., Chatham Co, GA[15, 19].

More About Mack Mason:
b: May 06, 1879 in Davisboro, Washington, GA[15]
Census: 1880 in Davisboro, Washington, GA
b: May 06, 1880[14]
Census: 1900 in Davisboro, Washington, GA[22]
Residence: 1907 in Batow 85th Dt., Jefferson Co, GA[23]
Tax:[24]
Residence: 1910 in ? Rhodes Rd., Savannah, GA
Occupation: Laborer (Stable)[25]
Census: 1910 in Louisville, Jefferson Co, GA[18]
Occupation: Farmer (General farm)[26]
Residence: 1920 in Road from Wadley to Pressluck?, Jefferson, GA[27]
Census: 1920 in Wadley, Jefferson, GA[26]
Residence: 1930 in 145 Lathorp Ave, Savannah, GA[28]
Census: 1930 in District 8, Chatham Co, GA (Mary)[29]

Occupation: Laborer (? plant)[28]
Residence: 1930 in 145 Lathorpe (Oglethorpe) Ave., Savannah, GA
Residence: 1938 in 1350 Augusta Rd., Savannah, Chatham Co, GA[19]
Census: 1940 in Savannah, Chatham Co, GA[30]
Occupation: Unemployed[31]
Residence: 1943 in 6 W. Exley St., Newtown, Savannah, GA[31]
Residence: 1949 in Savannah, Chatham Co, GA[14]
Social Security Number: 258-34-9996[32]
Funeral:[15]
Occupation: Retired Logger[15]
Residence: 1962 in 1109 Richard St., Savannah, Chatham Co, GA[15, 17]
Burial: September 22, 1962 in Oak Grove Cemetery, Savannah, Chatham Co, GA[15]
Occupation: Wood cutter (Pulp Wood Yard)[30]

Notes for Mack Mason:
Listed as MAXON [1910 Census]

More About Sarah "Sallie" A Shalteen Thompson:
Occupation: Servant[33]
Census: 1900 in Davisboro, Washington Co, GA[33]
Census: 1910 in Louisville, Jefferson Co, GA[18]
Occupation: Laundress[18]
Census: 1920 in Wadley, Jefferson Co, GA[34]
Residence: 1930 in 145 Lathorp Ave, Savannah, GA
Census: 1930 in District 8, Chatham Co, GA[35]
Occupation: Domestic[19]
Funeral:
Burial: March 31, 1938 in Lincoln Cemetery, Chatham Co, GA[19]
Cause Of Death: Cervix cancer[19]

Notes for Sarah "Sallie" A Shalteen Thompson:
Sarah (Sallie Anne) was named for her grandmother Sallie Mogran and probably from her mother Anne [author,1990]

Sarah "Sallie" A Shalteen Thompson and Mack Mason had the following children:
      i.   Jesse Mason (son of Mack Mason and Sarah "Sallie" A Shalteen

Thompson) was born in 1904 in GA.

    ii. John Dooly Mason (son of Mack Mason and Sarah "Sallie" A Shalteen Thompson) was born in 1906 in GA.

    iii. Anne Lee Mason (daughter of Mack Mason and Sarah "Sallie" A Shalteen Thompson) was born in 1907 in GA. She married ? Green. She married ? Harris.

    iv. Maria Mason (daughter of Mack Mason and Sarah "Sallie" A Shalteen Thompson) was born in 1910 in GA.

2.   v. Ned "Eddie" Mazo (son of Mack Mason and Sarah "Sallie" A Shalteen Thompson) was born on September 07, 1912 in Jefferson Co, GA. He died on December 20, 1997 in Sumter Regional Hospital, Americus, Sumter Co, GA[1, 2]. He met Delores Ann Curry, daughter of Robert J Washington Forsythe and Lucretia "Cressie" Jo Curry. She was born on February 24, 1948 in Savannah, Chatham Co, GA[3, 4]. She died on December 16, 2000 in Chestnut Hill, Philadelphia, PA. He married ? about 1940. He married Lucretia "Cressie" Jo Curry about 1950[10], daughter of Frederick "Freddie" Curry and Elizabeth Brown. She was born on March 05, 1929 in Savannah, Chatham Co, GA[36, 37]. She died on December 10, 1998 in Liberty Regional Medical Center, Hinesville, Liberty Co, GA[38]. He met Living Mazo, daughter of Ned "Eddie" Mazo and Lucretia "Cressie" Jo Curry. She was born about 1954.

    vi. Mack Mason (son of Mack Mason and Sarah "Sallie" A Shalteen Thompson) was born in 1914 in GA.

    vii. Robert B Mason (son of Mack Mason and Sarah "Sallie" A Shalteen Thompson) was born in 1923 in GA.

    viii. George Mason (son of Mack Mason and Sarah "Sallie" A Shalteen Thompson) was born in 1926 in GA.

    ix. Melvin Mason (son of Mack Mason and Sarah "Sallie" A Shalteen Thompson) was born in 1927 in Wadley, Jefferson Co, GA. He died after 1944.

6. **Robert J Washington Forsythe**, son of Percy Campbell Forsythe and Nina Washington was born on September 15, 1925 in Savannah, Chatham Co,

GA[39, 40, 41]. He died on November 22, 1999 in Seattle, King Co, WA[41, 42]. He married **Lucretia "Cressie" Jo Curry** on April 17, 1948 in Savannah, Chatham Co, GA[43].

7. **Lucretia "Cressie" Jo Curry**, daughter of Frederick "Freddie" Curry and Elizabeth Brown was born on March 05, 1929 in Savannah, Chatham Co, GA[36, 37]. She died on December 10, 1998 in Liberty Regional Medical Center, Hinesville, Liberty Co, GA[38].

More About Robert J Washington Forsythe:
b: June 15, 1925 in Daufuskie, Beaufort Co, SC[44]
Census: 1930 in Savannah, Chatham Co, GA[45]
Residence: 1930 in 120 Randolph St., Savannah, GA
Census: 1940 in Savannah, Chatham Co, GA[46]
Military Service: Bet. November 13, 1942-November 15, 1945[47]
Residence: 1944 in 124 Reynolds St.[48]
Social Security Number: 259-40-7505[40]
Residence: 1945 in ?61 Indian St., Savannah, GA[40]
Residence: 1969 in Seattle, King Co, WA[44]
Residence: 1999 in Seattle, King Co, WA[49]
Burial: December 07, 1999 in Tahoma National Cemetery, St. Kent, King Co, WA[50]

Notes for Robert J Washington Forsythe:
Robert Washington Forsythe was possibly named after his father who occasionally listed as Robert Percy and his grandfather Joe Washington [author,1990]

Born Daufuskie Island, Beaufort, SC [Robert Forsythe, SS-5 application, Application for SSN, Social Security Administration, 1945]

More About Lucretia "Cressie" Jo Curry:
Census: 1930
Census: 1940 in Savannah, Chatham Co, GA[51]
Occupation: Domestic cook?[13]
Residence: Bet. 1965-1966 in 1936 Dennie St., Philadelphia, PA[52, 53]
Social Security Number: 202-40-5156[37, 54]
Funeral:
Residence: 1998 in Midway, Liberty, GA[55]

Burial: December 15, 1998 in Midway Cong. Cemetery, Midway, Liberty Co, GA[38]
Occupation: Homemaker[38]

Notes for Lucretia "Cressie" Jo Curry:
Cressie Jo was named for her great-grandmother, Lucretia (Cressie) and her grandfather Joe Brown [author,1990]

Born 1930 & Died 12/10/1998, [Cressie Curry, December 1998, issued PA, resided GA, Social Security Death Index, www.ancestry.com]

Lucretia "Cressie" Jo Curry and Robert J Washington Forsythe had the following child:

3.   i.   Delores Ann Curry (daughter of Robert J Washington Forsythe and Lucretia "Cressie" Jo Curry) was born on February 24, 1948 in Savannah, Chatham Co, GA[3, 4]. She died on December 16, 2000 in Chestnut Hill, Philadelphia, PA. She met Ned "Eddie" Mazo, son of Mack Mason and Sarah "Sallie" A Shalteen Thompson. He was born on September 07, 1912 in Jefferson Co, GA. He died on December 20, 1997 in Sumter Regional Hospital, Americus, Sumter Co, GA[1, 2]. She married Living Williams.

Generation 4

8.   **Edward "Ned" Mason**, son of Alfred Mason and Hannah ? was born in 1847 in Washington Co, GA[56]. He died between 1888-1900 in Washington Co?, GA. He married **Ranie Brown** about 1869 in Washington Co, GA.

9.   **Ranie Brown**, daughter of George Brown and May A ? was born in December 1852 in Washington Co, GA[56, 57]. She died between 1910-1920 in Washington Co?, GA.

More About Edward "Ned" Mason:
Census: 1870 in Davisboro, Washington, GA[58]
Occupation: Farm laborer[59]
Occupation: Farmer[60, 61]
Census: 1880 in Davisboro, Washington, GA[60, 61]
Residence: 1888 in 200 Broughton, Savannah, Chatham Co, GA[62]
Occupation: Clk [Clerk][62]

More About Ranie Brown:
Occupation: Keeping house[59]
Census: 1870 in Davisboro, Washington, GA[63]
Occupation: K. house[60, 61]
Census: 1880 in Davisboro, Washington, GA[64]
Census: 1900 in Davisboro, Washington, GA[22]
Occupation: Washwoman[22]
Census: 1910 in Davisboro, Washington, GA[25]
Occupation: Washer woman[25]

Notes for Ranie Brown:
Ranie was probably named for her grandmother Rhinor [author, 2005]

Born 1849 [1870 Census]

Surname aka Bryant, aka Rhina [author, 2003]

Ranie Brown and Edward "Ned" Mason had the following children:

    i.   George W Mason (son of Edward "Ned" Mason and Ranie Brown) was born in 1869 in GA. He married Hilda ?. She was born in 1870 in GA. He married Lavinia ? on December 24, 1897. She was born in 1866 in GA.

    ii.   James Mason (son of Edward "Ned" Mason and Ranie Brown) was born in 1872 in GA.

    iii.   Aggie Mason (daughter of Edward "Ned" Mason and Ranie Brown) was born on March 10, 1872 in Washington Co, GA[65]. She died in 1922 in Ivey, Johnson Co, GA[65]. She married William? Palmer.

    iv.   Plum Mason (daughter of Edward "Ned" Mason and Ranie Brown) was born in 1874 in GA.

    v.   Jane Mason (daughter of Edward "Ned" Mason and Ranie Brown) was born in 1875 in GA.

    vi.   Dicey Mason (child of Edward "Ned" Mason and Ranie Brown) was born in 1876 in GA.

    vii.   Austin Mason (son of Edward "Ned" Mason and Ranie Brown) was born in 1878 in GA. He married Leila Wicker on December

09, 1905[66].

4. viii Mack Mason (son of Edward "Ned" Mason and Ranie Brown)
. was born on September 25, 1880 in Washington Co, GA[14]. He
died on September 18, 1962 in Daughter Annie's Home,
Savannah, Chatham Co, GA[15, 16, 17]. He married Sarah "Sallie" A
Shalteen Thompson on December 15, 1902 in Washington Co,
GA[18, 19, 20], daughter of Peter Thompson and Anne Shatteen. She
was born in June 1883 in Washington Co, GA[18, 19, 21]. She died
on March 21, 1938 in Augusta Rd., Chatham Co, GA[15, 19].

ix. Alonzo Mason (son of Edward "Ned" Mason and Ranie Brown)
was born in 1882 in GA. He married Martha Ann Clayton on
December 16, 1897[67]. She was born about 1880.

x. Janice Mason (daughter of Edward "Ned" Mason and Ranie
Brown) was born in 1885 in GA.

xi. Ella Mason (daughter of Edward "Ned" Mason and Ranie
Brown) was born in 1886 in GA.

xii. Oliver Mason (son of Edward "Ned" Mason and Ranie Brown)
was born in 1888 in GA.

10. **Peter Thompson**, son of Stephen Thompson and Nancy ? was born in
February 1860 in Jefferson Co, GA[19, 68]. He died between 1900-1910 in
GA?. He married **Anne Shatteen** on May 19, 1881 in Washington Co, GA[69].

11. **Anne Shatteen**, daughter of Mason Shatteen and Sallie Morgan was born
about 1865 in Washington Co, GA[19]. She died between 1884-1900 in GA?.

More About Peter Thompson:
Census: 1870
Occupation: Laborer[70]
Census: 1880 in Davisboro, Washington Co, GA[70]
Occupation: Farm laborer[68]
Census: 1900 in Grange, Jefferson Co, GA[68]

Notes for Peter Thompson:
May have remarried in 1888, Georgia Givins [author, 2004]

More About Anne Shatteen:
Census: 1870

Occupation: Laborer[71]
Census: 1880 in Davisboro, Washington Co, GA[71]

Notes for Anne Shatteen:
aka Shelton

Anne Shatteen and Peter Thompson had the following child:

5.   i.   Sarah "Sallie" A Shalteen Thompson (daughter of Peter Thompson and Anne Shatteen) was born in June 1883 in Washington Co, GA[18, 19, 21]. She died on March 21, 1938 in Augusta Rd., Chatham Co, GA[15, 19]. She married Mack Mason on December 15, 1902 in Washington Co, GA[18, 19, 20], son of Edward "Ned" Mason and Ranie Brown. He was born on September 25, 1880 in Washington Co, GA[14]. He died on September 18, 1962 in Daughter Annie's Home, Savannah, Chatham Co, GA[15, 16, 17].

12.   **Percy Campbell Forsythe**, son of Theodore (Theopolis) Forsythe and Margaret ? was born in January 1882 in Bahamas, West Indies (Eng)[72]. He died on January 19, 1942 in Chatham Co, GA[73]. He married **Nina Washington** about 1923 in GA?.

13.   **Nina Washington**, daughter of Joseph "Joe" Washington and Mary Robinson was born on October 31, 1908 in Daufuskie, Beaufort Co, SC[48, 74]. She died on August 05, 1944 in Charity Hospital, Savannah, Chatham Co, GA[48, 74, 75].

More About Percy Campbell Forsythe:
Immigration: Abt. 1886 in West Indies to Florida[76]
Occupation: Laborer (day)[72]
Residence: 1900 in Pippins St., Jacksonville, FL[72]
Census: 1900 in Jacksonville, Duval Co, FL[72]
Occupation: Waiter (Hotel)[77]
Census: 1910 in Jacksonville, Duval Co, FL[77]
Residence: 1910 in 933 Odessa St., Jacksonville, FL[77]
Census: 1920
Residence: 1930 in 413/913 59th St., Washington DC[78]
Occupation: Laborer[78]
Census: 1930 in Washington DC[78]
Residence: 1930 in 413 59th St., Washington DC

Census: 1940 in Savannah, Chatham Co, GA[46]
Occupation: Messman (SS City of Atlanta)[79]
Military Service: 1942[79, 80]
Probate: April 07, 1942 in Chatham Co, GA[73]
Cause Of Death: Lost his life on SS City of Atlanta, sunk by enemy torpedo[73]
Occupation: Meat cook (Srteam ship)[46]

Notes for Percy Campbell Forsythe:
Also Robert Percy

More About Nina Washington:
Census: 1910 in Savannah, Chatham Co, GA[81]
Census: 1920 in Savannah, Chatham Co, GA[82]
Residence: 1920 in 321 Bay St., Savannah, Chatham Co, GA
Residence: 1930 in 120 Randolph St., Savannah, GA
Census: 1930 in Savannah, Chatham Co, GA[45]
Census: 1940 in Savannah, Chatham Co, GA[46]
Residence: 1944 in Springfield Plantation, Chatham Co, GA[75]
Occupation: Domestic[48]
Burial: August 09, 1944 in Laurel Grove Cemetery, Savannah, Chatham Co, GA[74]
Probate: October 11, 1944 in Chatham Co, GA[75]
Occupation: Cook helper (restaurant)[46]
Cause Of Death: Difficult Labor w/mitral insufficiency[48]

Notes for Nina Washington:
Born GA [ccording to records, an infant Forsyth died 8/5/1944, 4 days before Nina died. Possible she died after death of her infant; Nina Washington Forsyth, Cemetery Record, City of Savannah, Cemeteries Dept., Savannah, GA c/o Jerry Flemming, Director of Cemeteries]

Lived with a Mary Robinson and Mary Dunham (Dunbar) that may be the same woman and may be her mother. Also a Cornelia (Caroline) Warn (Warren) of grandmother with family. [author, 2003]

Nina Washington and Percy Campbell Forsythe had the following children:
      i.   Nina Forsythe (daughter of Percy Campbell Forsythe and Nina

Washington) was born about 1923 in GA. She died on December 05, 2000 in Tampa, Hillsborough Co, FL.

ii. Mildred Forsythe (daughter of Percy Campbell Forsythe and Nina Washington) was born about 1924 in GA?. She married ? Howard.

6.   iii. Robert J Washington Forsythe (son of Percy Campbell Forsythe and Nina Washington) was born on September 15, 1925 in Savannah, Chatham Co, GA[39, 40, 41]. He died on November 22, 1999 in Seattle, King Co, WA[41, 42]. He married Lucretia "Cressie" Jo Curry on April 17, 1948 in Savannah, Chatham Co, GA[43], daughter of Frederick "Freddie" Curry and Elizabeth Brown. She was born on March 05, 1929 in Savannah, Chatham Co, GA[36, 37]. She died on December 10, 1998 in Liberty Regional Medical Center, Hinesville, Liberty Co, GA[38].

14. **Frederick "Freddie" Curry**, son of Duncan C Curry and Elizabeth "Bessie" Alston was born on February 22, 1907 in Savannah, Chatham Co, GA[83, 84]. He died on November 13, 1964 in Savannah, Chatham Co, GA[83, 85]. He married **Elizabeth Brown** on September 17, 1928 in Savannah, Chatham Co, GA[86, 87].

15. **Elizabeth Brown**, daughter of Joseph "Joe" Brown and Nancy Frazier was born between 06-June 11, 1911 in Allendale, Barnwell (Allendale), SC[53]. She died on October 16, 1965 in Chatham Co, GA[53, 88].

More About Frederick "Freddie" Curry:
b: February 15, 1907 in Savannah, Chatham Co, GA[89]
Census: 1910 in Savannah, Chatham Co, GA[90]
Census: 1920 in Savannah, Chatham Co, GA[91]
Occupation: Laborer (? Plant)[86]
Residence: 1930 in 143 Lathorp Ave, Savannah, GA[92]
Residence: 1930 in 143 Lathrope (Oglethorpe) Ave., Savannah, GA
Census: 1930 in District 8, Chatham Co, GA[93]
Census: 1940 in Savannah, Chatham Co, GA[51]
Social Security Number: 255-05-5233[83]
Residence: 1964 in 1108 Rogers Street, Newtown, GA[83]
Residence: 1964 in Savannah, Chatham Co, GA[84]
Occupation: Laborer (Tobacco Farm)[83]

Funeral:[83]
Burial: November 18, 1964 in Laurel Grove Cemetery, Savannah, Chatham Co, GA[83, 94]
Occupation: Cottom blocker (Cotton compress)[51]
Cause Of Death: Acute coronary occlusion[83]

More About Elizabeth Brown:
Census: 1920 in Allendale, Allendale Co, SC[95]
Census: 1930 in District 8, Chatham Co, GA
Residence: 1930 in 143 Lathorp Ave, Savannah, GA
Census: 1940 in Savannah, Chatham Co, GA[51]
Occupation: Housewife[53]
Funeral:[53, 96]
Residence: 1965 in 1108 Rogers St., Savannah, Chatham Co, GA[53, 96]
Burial: October 20, 1965 in Laurel Grove Cemetery, Savannah, Chatham Co, GA[53, 97]
Cause Of Death: Cerebral hemorrhage[53]
Occupation: Homemaker

Notes for Elizabeth Brown:
Grandmother Barnes born 1885 SC

Elizabeth Brown and Frederick "Freddie" Curry had the following children:

7.   i.   Lucretia "Cressie" Jo Curry (daughter of Frederick "Freddie" Curry and Elizabeth Brown) was born on March 05, 1929 in Savannah, Chatham Co, GA[36, 37]. She died on December 10, 1998 in Liberty Regional Medical Center, Hinesville, Liberty Co, GA[38]. She married Robert J Washington Forsythe on April 17, 1948 in Savannah, Chatham Co, GA[43], son of Percy Campbell Forsythe and Nina Washington. He was born on September 15, 1925 in Savannah, Chatham Co, GA[39, 40, 41]. He died on November 22, 1999 in Seattle, King Co, WA[41, 42]. She married Ned "Eddie" Mazo about 1950[10], son of Mack Mason and Sarah "Sallie" A Shalteen Thompson. Hc was born on September 07, 1912 in Jefferson Co, GA. He died on December 20, 1997 in Sumter Regional Hospital, Americus, Sumter Co, GA[1, 2].

        ii.   Nancy Curry (daughter of Frederick "Freddie" Curry and Elizabeth Brown) was born in 1930 in GA. She died in 1964.

  iii. Frank Curry (son of Frederick "Freddie" Curry and Elizabeth Brown) was born about 1935 in GA.

  iv. Samuel Curry (son of Frederick "Freddie" Curry and Elizabeth Brown) was born about 1935 in GA.

  v. William Curry (son of Frederick "Freddie" Curry and Elizabeth Brown) was born about 1935 in GA.

  vi. Frederick "Fred" Curry (son of Frederick "Freddie" Curry and Elizabeth Brown) was born on August 18, 1936 in GA. He died on June 04, 1999 in Jacksonville, Duval Co, FL.

Generation 5

16. **Alfred Mason**, son of Moses? Mason and ? was born between 1825-1830 in GA. He died between 1880-1900 in Washington Co?, GA. He married **Hannah ?** about 1846 in GA.

17. **Hannah ?**, daughter of ? and ? was born in 1829 in GA. She died between 1900-1910 in Washington Co?, GA.

More About Alfred Mason:
Occupation: Farming[58]
Census: 1870 in Cato, Washington, GA[58]
Occupation: Farmer[61]
Census: 1880 in Cato, Washington, GA[98]

Notes for Alfred Mason:
Living with Augusta Neal, born GA, age c 82 or other, possible FIL [Neal household, 1880 United States Census, Washington, GA, ancestry.com & Microfilm, PA State Library, Hbg, PA]

Mason: Spanish: nickname for a forceful person or metonymic occupational name for someone who used a mallet, Spanish mazo (a byform of Maza 1). Spanish (from Galician and Asturian-Leonese): habitational name from any of a number of places so named in Galicia, Asturies, and Lleón. English and Scottish: occupational name for a stonemason, Middle English, Old French mas(s)on. Stonemasonry was a hugely important craft in the Middle Ages. Italian (Veneto): from a short form of Masone. French: from a regional variant of maison 'house'.

More About Hannah ?:
Census: 1870 in Cato, Washington, GA[58]
Occupation: Keeping house[58, 61]
Census: 1880 in Cato, Washington, GA[98]
Census: 1900 in Cato, Washington, GA[22]

Hannah ? and Alfred Mason had the following children:

8.   i.   Edward "Ned" Mason (son of Alfred Mason and Hannah ?) was born in 1847 in Washington Co, GA[56]. He died between 1888-1900 in Washington Co?, GA. He married Ranie Brown about 1869 in Washington Co, GA, daughter of George Brown and May A ?. She was born in December 1852 in Washington Co, GA[56, 57]. She died between 1910-1920 in Washington Co?, GA.

    ii.   Noah Mason (son of Alfred Mason and Hannah ?) was born in 1848 in GA.

    iii.   Thomas Mason (son of Alfred Mason and Hannah ?) was born in 1853 in GA. He married Pheobe Walker on May 02, 1874[99]. She was born in 1852 in GA.

    iv.   James? Mason (son of Alfred Mason and Hannah ?) was born about 1855 in GA.

    v.   Linda Mason (daughter of Alfred Mason and Hannah ?) was born in 1856 in GA. She married Daniel Middleton in 1878. He was born about 1855 in GA.

    vi.   Andrew Mason (son of Alfred Mason and Hannah ?) was born in 1857 in GA. He married Ellen Walker on June 22, 1871[99]. She was born in 1850.

    vii.   Jacob "Jake" Mason (son of Alfred Mason and Hannah ?) was born in 1859 in GA. He married Ellen Adams on November 18, 1876[100]. She was born in 1859 in GA.

    viii.   George Mason (son of Alfred Mason and Hannah ?) was born in 1861 in GA. He married Charlotte Andrews on May 27, 1882[101].

    ix.   Jefferson D Mason (son of Alfred Mason and Hannah ?) was born in 1862 in GA. He married Carrie Moffett in 1894[102].

    x.   Josephine Mason (daughter of Alfred Mason and Hannah ?) was born in 1864 in GA. She married King Reeves?.

xi. Alfred Mason (son of Alfred Mason and Hannah ?) was born in 1868 in GA. He married Harriet Cumming on November 25, 1886[103].

xii. Cleveland Mason (son of Alfred Mason and Hannah ?) was born in 1870 in GA.

18. **George Brown**, son of Samuel? Brown and Rhinor? ? was born about 1822 in GA[104]. He died after 1870 in GA. He married **May A ?** about 1851 in GA.

19. **May A ?** was born about 1836 in GA[104]. She died after 1870 in GA.

More About George Brown:
Occupation: Farmer[104]
Census: 1870 in Davisboro, Washington Co, GA[104]
Census: 1880

Notes for George Brown:
Brown: English, Scottish, and Irish: generally a nickname referring to the color of the hair or complexion, Middle English br(o)un, from Old English brun or Old French brun. This word is occasionally found in Old English and Old Norse as a personal name or byname. Brun- was also a Germanic name-forming element. Some instances of Old English Brun as a personal name may therefore be short forms of compound names such as Brungar, Brunwine, etc. As a Scottish and Irish name, it sometimes represents a translation of Gaelic Donn. As an American family name, it has absorbed numerous surnames from other languages with the same meaning.

More About May A ?:
Occupation: Keeping house[104]
Census: 1870 in Davisboro, Washington Co, GA[104]
Census: 1880

May A ? and George Brown had the following children:
9.   i.   Ranie Brown (daughter of George Brown and May A ?) was born in December 1852 in Washington Co, GA[56, 57]. She died between 1910-1920 in Washington Co?, GA. She married Edward "Ned" Mason about 1869 in Washington Co, GA, son of Alfred Mason and Hannah ?. He was born in 1847 in

Washington Co, GA[56]. He died between 1888-1900 in Washington Co?, GA.

    ii. Rachel Brown (daughter of George Brown and May A ?) was born in 1854 in GA.

    iii. Samuel Brown (son of George Brown and May A ?) was born in 1856 in GA.

    iv. Simon Brown (son of George Brown and May A ?) was born in 1857 in GA.

    v. Mary Brown (daughter of George Brown and May A ?) was born in 1861 in GA.

    vi. Remus Brown (son of George Brown and May A ?) was born in 1863 in GA.

20. **Stephen Thompson**, son of Samuel? Thompson and ? was born about 1820 in SC (GA?)[105]. He died after 1879 in GA?. He married **Nancy ?** about 1859 in Chatham Co, GA?.

21. **Nancy ?**, daughter of ? and ? was born about 1841 in NC (GA/SC)[105]. She died after 1879 in GA?.

More About Stephen Thompson:
Occupation: Farm laborer[105]
Census: 1870 in Dt 5, Savannah, Chatham Co, GA[105]
Occupation: Farmer[106]
Census: 1880 in Dt 8, Chatham Co, GA[106]

More About Nancy ?:
Census: 1870 in Dt 5, Savannah, Chatham Co, GA[105]
Occupation: Keeping house[106]

Nancy ? and Stephen Thompson had the following children:

10. i. Peter Thompson (son of Stephen Thompson and Nancy ?) was born in February 1860 in Jefferson Co, GA[19, 68]. He died between 1900-1910 in GA?. He married Anne Shatteen on May 19, 1881 in Washington Co, GA[69], daughter of Mason Shatteen and Sallie Morgan. She was born about 1865 in Washington Co, GA[19]. She died between 1884-1900 in GA?.

    ii. Seymour Thompson (son of Stephen Thompson and Nancy ?)

was born in 1865 in GA.

- iii. Julia Thompson (daughter of Stephen Thompson and Nancy ?) was born about 1867 in GA.

- iv. Layer Thompson (daughter of Stephen Thompson and Nancy ?) was born about 1869 in GA.

- v. Cato C Thompson (son of Stephen Thompson and Nancy ?) was born in 1869 in GA. He married Flander A Mason in 1902[107].

- vi. Joshua A Thompson (son of Stephen Thompson and Nancy ?) was born in 1870 in GA. He married Mary Chapman.

- vii. Henry Thompson (son of Stephen Thompson and Nancy ?) was born about 1872 in GA.

- viii. J J Thompson (son of Stephen Thompson and Nancy ?) was born about 1872 in GA. He married Mary Key in 1896[108].

- ix. Cornelius Thompson (son of Stephen Thompson and Nancy ?) was born about 1874 in GA.

- x. Stephen Thompson (son of Stephen Thompson and Nancy ?) was born in 1879 in GA.

22. **Mason Shatteen**, son of ? Shateen and ? was born about 1835 in GA. He died between 1880-1900 in GA?. He married **Sallie Morgan** about 1861 in GA.

23. **Sallie Morgan**, daughter of Thomas Morgan and ? was born in March 1847 in Davisboro, Washington Co, GA[33, 109]. She died on November 10, 1927 in Savannah, Chatham Co, GA[109, 110].

More About Mason Shatteen:
Census: 1870
Occupation: Farmer[71]
Census: 1880 in Davisboro, Washington Co, GA[71]

More About Sallie Morgan:
Census: 1870
Occupation: K house[71]
Census: 1880 in Davisboro, Washington Co, GA[71]
Occupation: Servant[21]
Census: 1900 in Davisboro, Washington Co, GA[21]

Census: 1910 in Militia Dt 85, Jefferson Co, GA[111]
Census: 1920 in Savannah, Chatham Co, GA[112]
Residence: 1920 in Church St., Savannah, Chatham Co, GA[112]
Occupation: Domestic[109]
Residence: 1927 in 440 Eagle St., Savannah, Chatham Co, GA[109]
Burial: November 13, 1927 in Laurel Grove Cemetery, Savannah, Chatham Co, GA[109]
Funeral:[109]
Cause Of Death: Chronic myocarditis[109]

Sallie Morgan and Mason Shatteen had the following children:

   i. Linnie Shatteen (daughter of Mason Shatteen and Sallie Morgan) was born in 1862 in GA.

11. ii. Anne Shatteen (daughter of Mason Shatteen and Sallie Morgan) was born about 1865 in Washington Co, GA[19]. She died between 1884-1900 in GA?. She married Peter Thompson on May 19, 1881 in Washington Co, GA[69], son of Stephen Thompson and Nancy ?. He was born in February 1860 in Jefferson Co, GA[19, 68]. He died between 1900-1910 in GA?.

   iii. James Shatteen (son of Mason Shatteen and Sallie Morgan) was born in 1866 in GA. He married Lula "Lou" ?. She was born in 1872 in GA. He married Susan Hall on December 27, 1889[113].

   iv. Lillie Shatteen (daughter of Mason Shatteen and Sallie Morgan) was born in 1868 in GA.

24. **Theodore (Theopolis) Forsythe**, son of Nelson Forsythe and Elizabeth Hapton was born between March 1855-1856 in West Indies (Eng)[77, 114]. He died on May 23, 1919 in Brunswick, Glynn Co, GA[114]. He married **Margaret ?** about 1881 in West Indies (Eng)[72].

25. **Margaret ?**, daughter of ? and ? was born between January 1865-1870 in West Indies (Eng)[78]. She died between 1930-1940.

More About Theodore (Theopolis) Forsythe:
Immigration: Abt. 1886 in West Indies to Florida[72]
Census: 1900 in Jacksonville, Duval Co, FL[72]
Residence: 1900 in Pippins St., Jacksonville, FL[72]
Occupation: Waiter (Hotel)[72, 77]

Residence: 1910 in 933 Odessa St., Jacksonville, FL[77]
Census: 1910 in Jacksonville, Duval Co, FL[77]
Residence: 1919 in 1314 Egmond St, Brook?, Glynn Co, GA[114]
Occupation: Laborer[114]
Burial: May 1919 in Greenwood Cemetery[114]
Funeral:[114]
Cause Of Death: Appolplexy [sic][114]

Notes for Theodore (Theopolis) Forsythe:
Death records lists death in Bwk(?), assume is Brunswick, Glynn Co, GA
[author, 2003]

More About Margaret ?:
Immigration: Bef. 1900
Occupation: Servant[72]
Census: 1900 in Jacksonville, Duval Co, FL[72]
Occupation: Laundress[77]
Census: 1910 in Jacksonville, Duval Co, FL[77]
Census: 1920
Residence: 1930 in 413/913 59th St., Washington DC[78]
Census: 1930 in Washington DC[78]

Notes for Margaret ?:
May have passed Dec 29 1936, Fulton, GA

Margaret ? and Theodore (Theopolis) Forsythe had the following children:

12. i.   Percy Campbell Forsythe (son of Theodore (Theopolis) Forsythe and Margaret ?) was born in January 1882 in Bahamas, West Indies (Eng)[72]. He died on January 19, 1942 in Chatham Co, GA[73]. He married Nina Washington about 1923 in GA?, daughter of Joseph "Joe" Washington and Mary Robinson. She was born on October 31, 1908 in Daufuskie, Beaufort Co, SC[48, 74]. She died on August 05, 1944 in Charity Hospital, Savannah, Chatham Co, GA[48, 74, 75].

     ii.   Hattie Forsythe (daughter of Theodore (Theopolis) Forsythe and Margaret ?) was born in 1883 in West Indies (Eng).

     iii. Frederick Forsythe (son of Theodore (Theopolis) Forsythe and Margaret ?) was born in 1884 in West Indies (Eng).

iv. Theodore Forsythe (son of Theodore (Theopolis) Forsythe and Margaret ?) was born in 1886 in West Indies (Eng). He married Stella ?. She was born in 1885 in VA.

26. **Joseph "Joe" Washington**, son of Joseph "Joe" Washington and Tena ? was born between September 1868-1870 in Daufuskie, Beaufort Co, SC[48, 115, 116]. He died on November 30, 1922 in Gray's Hill, Beaufort Co, SC[116]. He met **Mary Robinson**.

27. **Mary Robinson**, daughter of Robert Robinson and Hester ? was born in May 1870 in Hilton Head, Beaufort Co, SC[48, 115, 117, 118]. She died on April 29, 1939 in Savannah, Chatham Co, GA[118].

More About Joseph "Joe" Washington:
Census: 1870
Education: at school[119]
Occupation: Works on farm[120]
Census: 1880 in St. Helena Island, Beaurfort Co, SC[119, 120]
Census: 1900 in Beaufort, Beaufort Co, SC[115]
Occupation: Day laborer[121]
Census: 1910 in Beaufort, Beaufort Co, SC[122]
Census: 1920 in Beaufort, Beaufort Co, SC[122]
Occupation: Farm laborer[116]
Burial: December 01, 1922 in Gray's Hill, Beaufort Co, SC[116]
Cause Of Death: Pneumonia[116]

Notes for Joseph "Joe" Washington:
Joe was named for his father Joe Washington [author, 2005]

Joe is listed twice in 1880 Census, once with mother Tennia and also with uncle DC [Washington household, 1880 United States Census, Beaufort Co, SC, www,ancestry.com]

It seems likely Joe and Mary were never married [author, 2005]

More About Mary Robinson:
Census: 1880 in Hilton Head, Beaufort Co, SC[123]
Census: 1900 in Beaufort, Beaufort Co, SC[115]
Residence: 1910 in 3 E. Broad, Savannah, Chatham Co, GA[117]
Occupation: Proprietor (Boarding house)[117]

Census: 1910 in Savannah, Chatham Co, GA[117]
Occupation: Proprietor (Lunch room)[124]
Residence: 1920 in 321 Bay St., Savannah, Chatham Co, GA[124]
Census: 1920 in Savannah, Chatham Co, GA[124]
Residence: 1930 in 120 Randolph St., Savannah, GA
Census: 1930 in Savannah, Chatham Co, GA[125]
Residence: 1930 in 120 Reynolds St., Savannah, Chatham Co, GA[125]
Occupation: Cook (Boarding house)[125]
Burial: May 01, 1939 in Laurel Grove South Cemetery, Savannah, Chatham Co, GA[126]

More About Joseph "Joe" Washington and Mary Robinson:
Other-Begin:[115, 117]

Mary Robinson and Joseph "Joe" Washington had the following children:

    i. Albert Ernest Robinson Washington (son of Joseph "Joe" Washington and Mary Robinson) was born in 1896 in SC.

13.   ii. Nina Washington (daughter of Joseph "Joe" Washington and Mary Robinson) was born on October 31, 1908 in Daufuskie, Beaufort Co, SC[48, 74]. She died on August 05, 1944 in Charity Hospital, Savannah, Chatham Co, GA[48, 74, 75]. She married Percy Campbell Forsythe about 1923 in GA?, son of Theodore (Theopolis) Forsythe and Margaret ?. He was born in January 1882 in Bahamas, West Indies (Eng)[72]. He died on January 19, 1942 in Chatham Co, GA[73]. She married ? Durham about 1940.

    iii. Charles H Robinson Washington (son of Joseph "Joe" Washington and Mary Robinson) was born in 1909 in GA.

28. **Duncan C Curry**, son of Fortune Curry and Mary ? was born in May 1869 in Beaufort Co?, SC[127, 128]. He died on June 03, 1914 in Savannah, Chatham Co, GA[129, 130]. He married **Elizabeth "Bessie" Alston** about 1890 in GA (SC)[127].

29. **Elizabeth "Bessie" Alston**, daughter of Benjamin "Ben" Alston and Lucretia ? was born in December 1870 in Beaufort Co?, SC[127]. She died between 1920-1930 in Chatham Co?, GA.

More About Duncan C Curry:
Census: 1870 in St Peters, Beaufort Co, SC[131]

Census: 1880 in Lawnton, Hampton Co, SC[132]

Residence: 1890 in bds ss Indian Ln, 3d E. of canal, Savannah, Chatham Co, GA[133]

Census: 1900 in 1st Militia, Chatham Co, GA[127]

Occupation: RR Laborer[127]

Residence: 1909 in 619 W Lumber St., Savannah, Chatham Co, GA[134]

Occupation: Laborer (On wharf)[90]

Census: 1910 in Savannah, Chatham Co, GA[90]

Residence: 1910 in 610 Oglethorpe Ave, Savannah, GA

Residence: 1914 in 610 W. Williams St., Savannah, Chatham Co, GA[130]

Occupation: Laborer[135]

Burial: June 1914 in Laurel Grove Cemetery, Savannah, Chatham Co, GA[135]

Cause Of Death: Cerebral congestion and hemorrhage[135]

Notes for Duncan C Curry:
Also listed born SC [census recs]

More About Elizabeth "Bessie" Alston:
Census: 1880 in Lawnton, Hampton Co, SC[136]

Census: 1900 in 1st Militia, Chatham Co, GA[127]

Census: 1910 in Savannah, Chatham Co, GA[90]

Census: 1920 in Savannah, Chatham Co, GA[91]

Residence: 1926 in 6 Dermon? St., Savannah, Chatham Co, GA[128]

Notes for Elizabeth "Bessie" Alston:
Listed as mixed [1920 census]

Also listed born SC [census]

Elizabeth "Bessie" Alston and Duncan C Curry had the following children:

    i.   William "Willie" Curry (son of Duncan C Curry and Elizabeth "Bessie" Alston) was born in 1892 in GA. He married Nellie ?. She was born in 1894 in GA.

    ii.   Elizabeth "Bessie" Curry (daughter of Duncan C Curry and Elizabeth "Bessie" Alston) was born in 1894 in GA.

    iii.   Ira Curry (son of Duncan C Curry and Elizabeth "Bessie" Alston) was born in 1895 in GA.

    iv.   Rosa Louise Curry (daughter of Duncan C Curry and Elizabeth

"Bessie" Alston) was born about 1899 in Savannah, Chatham Co, GA[128]. She died in 1922 in Savannah, Chatham Co, GA[128].

v. Hilda Curry (daughter of Duncan C Curry and Elizabeth "Bessie" Alston) was born in 1899 in GA.

vi. Leola Curry (daughter of Duncan C Curry and Elizabeth "Bessie" Alston) was born in 1902 in GA.

vii. Solomon Curry (son of Duncan C Curry and Elizabeth "Bessie" Alston) was born in 1904 in GA. He married Anne ?. She was born in 1907.

viii. Edmonia Curry (daughter of Duncan C Curry and Elizabeth "Bessie" Alston) was born in 1906 in GA.

14. ix. Frederick "Freddie" Curry (son of Duncan C Curry and Elizabeth "Bessie" Alston) was born on February 22, 1907 in Savannah, Chatham Co, GA[83, 84]. He died on November 13, 1964 in Savannah, Chatham Co, GA[83, 85]. He married Elizabeth Brown on September 17, 1928 in Savannah, Chatham Co, GA[86, 87], daughter of Joseph "Joe" Brown and Nancy Frazier. She was born between 06-June 11, 1911 in Allendale, Barnwell (Allendale), SC[53]. She died on October 16, 1965 in Chatham Co, GA[53, 88].

x. Frampton Curry (son of Duncan C Curry and Elizabeth "Bessie" Alston) was born in 1909 in GA.

xi. Charles "Charlie" Curry (son of Duncan C Curry and Elizabeth "Bessie" Alston) was born on February 08, 1912 in GA. He died in April 1967 in Savannah, Chatham Co, GA.

30. **Joseph "Joe" Brown**, son of Joseph "Joe" Brown and Lina Glover? was born on July 05, 1890 in Allendale, Barnwell (Allendale) Co, SC[137, 138]. He died on December 13, 1942 in Chatham Co, GA[139]. He married **Nancy Frazier** about 1910 in Barnwell Co?, SC.

31. **Nancy Frazier**, daughter of Samuel "Sam" Frazier and Eva Thompson was born in 1889 in Barnwell Co, SC[137]. She died after 1940 in Chatham Co?, GA.

More About Joseph "Joe" Brown:
Census: 1900 in Allendale, Barnwell (Allendale), SC[140]

Residence: 1908 in Bill Exley farm, SC[137]
Occupation: Farm Labor (?)[141]
Census: 1910 in Allendale, Barnwell (Allendale), SC[141]
Occupation: Sawmill work (EF Woodward, Appleton, SC)[138]
Residence: 1920 in Johnson Landry Rd., Allendale Co, SC
Census: 1920 in Allendale, Allendale Co, SC[95]
Occupation: Farm Labor (Working out)[95]
Census: 1930 in District 8, Chatham Co, GA[142]
Occupation: Laborer (Barnell? Factory)[142]
Residence: 1930 in 142 Lathrope (Oglethorpe) Ave., Savannah, GA
Census: 1940 in Savannah, Chatham Co, GA[143]
Occupation: Laborer (Fertilizer plant)[143]
Medical Condition: Medium height, medium weight[138]

Notes for Joseph "Joe" Brown:
Joe was named for his father Joe Brown [author, 2005]

Also born GA [census recs]

Prob. buried 4/3/1951 [Laurel Grove South, Savannah, aged 65, b c 1886]

More About Nancy Frazier:
Census: 1900 in Bull Pond, Barnwell Co, SC[144]
Occupation: Farm Laborer[144]
Occupation: Farmer (Parents)[145]
Census: 1910 in Allendale, Barnwell (Allendale), SC[145]
Occupation: Farm Labor (Working out)[95]
Census: 1920 in Allendale, Allendale Co, SC[95]
Census: 1930 in District 8, Chatham Co, GA[142]
Census: 1940 in Savannah, Chatham Co, GA[143]

Nancy Frazier and Joseph "Joe" Brown had the following children:
15. i. Elizabeth Brown (daughter of Joseph "Joe" Brown and Nancy Frazier) was born between 06-June 11, 1911 in Allendale, Barnwell (Allendale), SC[53]. She died on October 16, 1965 in Chatham Co, GA[53, 88]. She married Frederick "Freddie" Curry on September 17, 1928 in Savannah, Chatham Co, GA[86, 87], son of Duncan C Curry and Elizabeth "Bessie" Alston. He was born on February 22, 1907 in Savannah, Chatham Co, GA[83, 84]. He died

on November 13, 1964 in Savannah, Chatham Co, GA[83, 85].

ii. Josephine Brown (daughter of Joseph "Joe" Brown and Nancy Frazier) was born in 1915 in SC.

iii. Christopher Columbus Brown (son of Joseph "Joe" Brown and Nancy Frazier) was born in 1916 in SC.

iv. Benjamin Brown (son of Joseph "Joe" Brown and Nancy Frazier) was born in 1919 in SC.

v. Dorothy Mae Brown (daughter of Joseph "Joe" Brown and Nancy Frazier) was born about 1920 in SC. She married ? Miller.

vi. Ellis Brown (son of Joseph "Joe" Brown and Nancy Frazier) was born about 1920 in SC.

vii. Lillian "Lillie" Brown (daughter of Joseph "Joe" Brown and Nancy Frazier) was born about 1920 in SC.

viii. Ella Lee Brown (daughter of Joseph "Joe" Brown and Nancy Frazier) was born on October 27, 1921 in SC. She died on December 08, 1999 in Atlanta, Fulton Co, GA. She married ? Gould.

ix. Adam Brown (son of Joseph "Joe" Brown and Nancy Frazier) was born in 1924 in SC.

x. Eva Mae Brown (daughter of Joseph "Joe" Brown and Nancy Frazier) was born on May 14, 1924 in SC. She died on April 07, 1988 in Savannah, Chatham Co, GA. She married ? Grant.

Generation 6

32. **Moses? Mason** was born about 1800 in GA. He married **?**.

33. **?** was born in GA.

Notes for ?:
Surname possible Neal [Neal hosuehold, 1880 United States Census, Washington, GA, ancestry.com & Microfilm, PA State Library, Hbg, PA]

? and Moses? Mason had the following child:

16. i. Alfred Mason (son of Moses? Mason and ?) was born between 1825-1830 in GA. He died between 1880-1900 in Washington Co?, GA. He married Hannah ? about 1846 in GA, daughter of ?

and ?. She was born in 1829 in GA. She died between 1900-1910 in Washington Co?, GA.

34. **?** was born in GA. He married **?**.

35. **?** was born in GA.

? and ? had the following child:

17.   i.   Hannah ? (daughter of ? and ?) was born in 1829 in GA. She died between 1900-1910 in Washington Co?, GA. She married Alfred Mason about 1846 in GA, son of Moses? Mason and ?. He was born between 1825-1830 in GA. He died between 1880-1900 in Washington Co?, GA.

36. **Samuel? Brown** was born about 1800. He married **Rhinor? ?**.

37. **Rhinor? ?** was born about 1800.

Rhinor? ? and Samuel? Brown had the following child:

18.   i.   George Brown (son of Samuel? Brown and Rhinor? ?) was born about 1822 in GA[104]. He died after 1870 in GA. He married May A ? about 1851 in GA. She was born about 1836 in GA[104]. She died after 1870 in GA.

40. **Samuel? Thompson** was born about 1805 in GA[106]. He died after 1820. He married **?**.

41. **?** was born in GA[106].

? and Samuel? Thompson had the following child:

20.   i.   Stephen Thompson (son of Samuel? Thompson and ?) was born about 1820 in SC (GA)[105]. He died after 1879 in GA?. He married Nancy ? about 1859 in Chatham Co, GA?, daughter of ? and ?. She was born about 1841 in NC (GA/SC)[105]. She died after 1879 in GA?.

42. **?** was born in GA[106]. He married **?**.

43. **?** was born in GA[106].

? and ? had the following child:

21.   i.   Nancy ? (daughter of ? and ?) was born about 1841 in NC (GA/SC)[105]. She died after 1879 in GA?. She married Stephen

Thompson about 1859 in Chatham Co, GA?, son of Samuel? Thompson and ?. He was born about 1820 in SC (GA)[105]. He died after 1879 in GA?.

44. **? Shateen** was born in GA. He married **?**.

45. **?** was born in GA.

? and ? Shateen had the following children:

22.   i.   Mason Shatteen (son of ? Shateen and ?) was born about 1835 in GA. He died between 1880-1900 in GA?. He married Sallie Morgan about 1861 in GA, daughter of Thomas Morgan and ?. She was born in March 1847 in Davisboro, Washington Co, GA[33, 109]. She died on November 10, 1927 in Savannah, Chatham Co, GA[109, 110].

       ii.   Isaac Shatteen (son of ? Shateen and ?) was born in 1842 in GA.

       iii.   Jesse Shatteen (son of ? Shateen and ?) was born in 1844 in GA.

       iv.   Virgil Shatteen (son of ? Shateen and ?) was born in 1844.

46. **Thomas Morgan** was born about 1820 in Davisboro, Washingtion Co, GA[109]. He died after 1857 in GA?. He married **?** about 1840.

47. **?** was born about 1820 in GA.

? and Thomas Morgan had the following child:

23.   i.   Sallie Morgan (daughter of Thomas Morgan and ?) was born in March 1847 in Davisboro, Washington Co, GA[33, 109]. She died on November 10, 1927 in Savannah, Chatham Co, GA[109, 110]. She married Mason Shatteen about 1861 in GA, son of ? Shateen and ?. He was born about 1835 in GA. He died between 1880-1900 in GA?.

48. **Nelson Forsythe** was born about 1820 in Nassau, Bahamas, West Indies (Eng)[114]. He died after 1856. He married **Elizabeth Hapton** about 1850.

49. **Elizabeth Hapton** was born about 1825 in West Indies (Eng). She died after 1856.

Elizabeth Hapton and Nelson Forsythe had the following child:

24.   i.   Theodore (Theopolis) Forsythe (son of Nelson Forsythe and

Elizabeth Hapton) was born between March 1855-1856 in West Indies (Eng)[77, 114]. He died on May 23, 1919 in Brunswick, Glynn Co, GA[114]. He married Margaret ? about 1881 in West Indies (Eng)[72], daughter of ? and ?. She was born between January 1865-1870 in West Indies (Eng)[78]. She died between 1930-1940.

50. **?** was born in West Indies (Eng). He married **?**.

51. **?** was born in West Indies (Eng).

? and ? had the following child:

   25.   i.   Margaret ? (daughter of ? and ?) was born between January 1865-1870 in West Indies (Eng)[78]. She died between 1930-1940. She married Theodore (Theopolis) Forsythe about 1881 in West Indies (Eng)[72], son of Nelson Forsythe and Elizabeth Hapton. He was born between March 1855-1856 in West Indies (Eng)[77, 114]. He died on May 23, 1919 in Brunswick, Glynn Co, GA[114].

52. **Joseph "Joe" Washington**, son of ? Washington and ? was born about 1835 in SC. He died after 1883 in SC?. He married **Tena ?** about 1855 in SC.

53. **Tena ?**, daughter of ? and ? was born about 1835 in SC. She died after 1883 in SC?.

More About Joseph "Joe" Washington:
Census: 1870
Census: 1880

More About Tena ?:
Census: 1870
Occupation: Keeps house[120]
Census: 1880 in St. Helena Island, Beaurfort Co, SC[120]
Census: 1900

Tena ? and Joseph "Joe" Washington had the following children:

   i.   Aaron Washington (son of Joseph "Joe" Washington and Tena ?) was born in 1860 in SC.

   ii.   Elizabeth "Betsy" Washington (daughter of Joseph "Joe" Washington and Tena ?) was born in 1864 in SC.

   iii.   Smart Washington (son of Joseph "Joe" Washington and Tena ?)

was born in 1866 in SC.

26.   iv.   Joseph "Joe" Washington (son of Joseph "Joe" Washington and Tena ?) was born between September 1868-1870 in Daufuskie, Beaufort Co, SC[48, 115, 116]. He died on November 30, 1922 in Gray's Hill, Beaufort Co, SC[116]. He met Mary Robinson, daughter of Robert Robinson and Hester ?. She was born in May 1870 in Hilton Head, Beaufort Co, SC[48, 115, 117, 118]. She died on April 29, 1939 in Savannah, Chatham Co, GA[118]. He married Flora ? about 1896 in SC. She was born about 1879 in SC.

v.   William Washington (son of Joseph "Joe" Washington and Tena ?) was born in 1883 in SC.

54.   **Robert Robinson**, son of ? Robinson and ? was born in July 1825 in SC[146, 147]. He died between 1900-1910 in SC. He married **Hester ?** about 1850 in Beaufort Co?, SC.

55.   **Hester ?**, daughter of ? and ? was born in May 1830 in SC[147]. She died between 1900-1910 in SC?.

More About Robert Robinson:
Census: 1870 in St. Lukes, Beaufort Co, SC[146]
Occupation: Farmer[123, 146, 147]
Census: 1880 in Hilton Head, Beaufort Co, SC[123]
Census: 1900 in Edisto Island, Charleston Co, SC[147]

More About Hester ?:
Census: 1870 in St. Lukes, Beaufort Co, SC[146]
Occupation: Keeping house[146]
Occupation: Farm laborer[123]
Census: 1880 in Hilton Head, Beaufort Co, SC[123]
Census: 1900 in Edisto Island, Charleston Co, SC[147]

Hester ? and Robert Robinson had the following children:

i.   Joseph Robinson (son of Robert Robinson and Hester ?) was born in 1855 in SC.

ii.   Emma Robinson (daughter of Robert Robinson and Hester ?) was born in 1857 in SC.

iii.   Elizabeth Robinson (daughter of Robert Robinson and Hester ?)

was born in 1863 in SC.

     iv. Dolly Robinson (daughter of Robert Robinson and Hester ?) was born in 1866 in SC.

27.   v. Mary Robinson (daughter of Robert Robinson and Hester ?) was born in May 1870 in Hilton Head, Beaufort Co, SC[48, 115, 117, 118]. She died on April 29, 1939 in Savannah, Chatham Co, GA[118]. She met Joseph "Joe" Washington, son of Joseph "Joe" Washington and Tena ?. He was born between September 1868-1870 in Daufuskie, Beaufort Co, SC[48, 115, 116]. He died on November 30, 1922 in Gray's Hill, Beaufort Co, SC[116]. She married ? Dunham.

    vi. Anna Robinson (daughter of Robert Robinson and Hester ?) was born in 1873 in SC.

    vii. Willis Robinson (son of Robert Robinson and Hester ?) was born in 1875 in SC.

    viii. John Robinson (son of Robert Robinson and Hester ?) was born in 1876 in SC.

56. **Fortune Curry** was born about 1815 in SC. He died between 1870-1880 in SC. He married **Mary ?** about 1850 in SC.

57. **Mary ?**, daughter of ? and ? was born about 1820 in SC. She died between 1880-1900 in SC.

More About Fortune Curry:
Occupation: Farm Labr[131]
Census: 1870 in St Peters, Beaufort Co, SC[131]

Notes for Fortune Curry:
Curry: Irish: Anglicized form of Gaelic Ó Comhraidhe, 'descendant of Comhraidhe', a personal name of uncertain meaning. Irish: Anglicized form of Gaelic Ó Corra (see Corr). Scottish and northern English: variant of Currie.

More About Mary ?:
Occupation: Farm labr[131]
Census: 1870 in St Peters, Beaufort Co, SC[131]

Census: 1880 in Lawnton, Hampton Co, SC[132]
Occupation: Farm laborer[132]

Mary ? and Fortune Curry had the following children:

      i.   Emma Curry (daughter of Fortune Curry and Mary ?) was born in 1854 in SC.

      ii.   Cyrus Curry (son of Fortune Curry and Mary ?) was born in 1859 in SC.

28.   iii. Duncan C Curry (son of Fortune Curry and Mary ?) was born in May 1869 in Beaufort Co?, SC[127, 128]. He died on June 03, 1914 in Savannah, Chatham Co, GA[129, 130]. He married Elizabeth "Bessie" Alston about 1890 in GA (SC)[127], daughter of Benjamin "Ben" Alston and Lucretia ?. She was born in December 1870 in Beaufort Co?, SC[127]. She died between 1920-1930 in Chatham Co?, GA.

58. **Benjamin "Ben" Alston**, son of ? Alston and ? was born in August 1845 in SC[148]. He died on August 15, 1918 in Savannah, Chatham Co, GA (SC)[139, 149]. He married **Lucretia ?** about 1863 in Beaufort Co?, SC.

59. **Lucretia ?**, daughter of ? and ? was born about 1840 in GA (SC). She died between 1880-1900 in SC.

More About Benjamin "Ben" Alston:
Census: 1870 in St. Peters, Beaufort Co, SC[150]
Occupation: Farmer[150, 151]
Census: 1880 in Lawnton, Hampton, SC[136]
Residence: 1890 in bds ss Indian Ln, 3d E. of canal, Savannah, Chatham Co, GA[152]
Occupation: Farm laborer[148]
Census: 1900 in Militia Dt 8, Chatham, GA[148]
Occupation: Farm laborer (Working out)
Census: 1910 in Militia Dt 8, Chatham, GA[153]
Burial: August 16, 1918 in Savannah, Chatham Co, GA[149]

More About Lucretia ?:
Occupation: Farm labor[150]
Census: 1870 in St. Peters, Beaufort Co, SC[150]
Census: 1880 in Lawnton, Hampton, SC[154]

Occupation: Labor[151]

Lucretia ? and Benjamin "Ben" Alston had the following children:

    i.   Lucy Alston (daughter of Benjamin "Ben" Alston and Lucretia ?) was born in 1865 in SC.

29. ii.   Elizabeth "Bessie" Alston (daughter of Benjamin "Ben" Alston and Lucretia ?) was born in December 1870 in Beaufort Co?, SC[127]. She died between 1920-1930 in Chatham Co?, GA. She married Duncan C Curry about 1890 in GA (SC)[127], son of Fortune Curry and Mary ?. He was born in May 1869 in Beaufort Co?, SC[127, 128]. He died on June 03, 1914 in Savannah, Chatham Co, GA[129, 130].

    iii.   Albert Alston (son of Benjamin "Ben" Alston and Lucretia ?) was born in 1874 in SC. He married Anna ?. She was born in 1883 in SC.

    iv.   Mary Alston (daughter of Benjamin "Ben" Alston and Lucretia ?) was born in 1878 in SC.

60. **Joseph "Joe" Brown**, son of David? Brown and Millie? Hay? was born in September 1871 in SC. He died between 1910-1920 in Barnwell Co?, SC. He married **Lina Glover?** about 1889 in Barnwell Co?, SC.

61. **Lina Glover?**, daughter of ? and ? was born in January 1872 in SC. She died between 1910-1920 in Barnwell Co?, SC.

More About Joseph "Joe" Brown:
Census: 1880
Occupation: Farmer[140]
Census: 1900 in Allendale, Barnwell (Allendale) Co, SC[140]
Census: 1910 in Allendale, Barnwell (Allendale) Co, SC[141]
Occupation: Farm Labor (General ?)[141]

Notes for Joseph "Joe" Brown:
Brown: English, Scottish, and Irish: generally a nickname referring to the color of the hair or complexion, Middle English br(o)un, from Old English brun or Old French brun. This word is occasionally found in Old English and Old Norse as a personal name or byname. Brun- was also a Germanic name-forming element. Some instances of Old English Brun as a personal name may therefore be short forms of compound names such as Brungar,

Brunwine, etc. As a Scottish and Irish name, it sometimes represents a translation of Gaelic Donn. As an American family name, it has absorbed numerous surnames from other languages with the same meaning.

More About Lina Glover?:
Census: 1880
Occupation: Farm laborer[140]
Census: 1900 in Allendale, Barnwell (Allendale), SC[140]
Census: 1910 in Allendale, Barnwell (Allendale), SC[141]
Occupation: ? (Odd jobs)[141]

Notes for Lina Glover?:
Surname possibly Barnes, b c1885 [author, 2008]

Lina Glover? and Joseph "Joe" Brown had the following children:

        i.   Linton Brown (son of Joseph "Joe" Brown and Lina Glover?) was born in 1889 in SC.

30.   ii.   Joseph "Joe" Brown (son of Joseph "Joe" Brown and Lina Glover?) was born on July 05, 1890 in Allendale, Barnwell (Allendale) Co, SC[137, 138]. He died on December 13, 1942 in Chatham Co, GA[139]. He married Nancy Frazier about 1910 in Barnwell Co?, SC, daughter of Samuel "Sam" Frazier and Eva Thompson. She was born in 1889 in Barnwell Co, SC[137]. She died after 1940 in Chatham Co?, GA.

      iii.   William Brown (son of Joseph "Joe" Brown and Lina Glover?) was born in 1892 in SC.

      iv.   Richard Brown (son of Joseph "Joe" Brown and Lina Glover?) was born in 1896 in SC.

62.   **Samuel "Sam" Frazier**, son of Smart Frazier and Minda Jones was born in July 1854 in Barnwell Co?, SC[144]. He died on March 19, 1928 in Chatham Co, GA[155]. He married **Eva Thompson** about 1879 in Barnwell Co?, SC.

63.   **Eva Thompson**, daughter of Adam Thompson and Mary ? was born in May 1860 in Allendale, Barnwell Co, SC[144, 156]. She died on January 25, 1929 in Mutual Quarters, Mil. 8, Chatham Co, GA[156, 157].

More About Samuel "Sam" Frazier:

Occupation: Farm laborer[158]
Census: 1870 in Allendale, Barnwell (Allendale), SC[158]
Occupation: Laborer[159]
Census: 1880 in Allendale, Barnwell (Allendale), SC[159]
Occupation: Farmer[144]
Census: 1900 in Bull Pond, Barnwell (Allendale), SC[144]
Occupation: Farmer (Private)[145]
Census: 1910 in Allendale, Barnwell (Allendale), SC[145]
Occupation: Farmer (General farm)[160]
Census: 1920 in Baldoc, Allendale Co, SC[160]
Residence: 1928 in 16 Lathrope Ave., Mutual Quarters, Chatham Co, GA[161]
Burial: March 21, 1928 in Laurel Grove Cemetery, Savannah, Chatham Co, GA[161]
Cause Of Death: Acute nephritis[161]

More About Eva Thompson:
Census: 1870 in Allendale, Barnwell Co, SC[162]
Census: 1880 in Allendale, Barnwell (Allendale), SC[159]
Occupation: Laborer[159]
Occupation: Farm laborer[144]
Census: 1900 in Bull Pond, Barnwell (Allendale), SC[144]
Census: 1910 in Allendale, Barnwell (Allendale), SC[145]
Census: 1920 in Baldoc, Allendale Co Co, SC[160]
Funeral:[156]
Burial: January 27, 1929 in Laurel Grove Cemetery, Savannah, Chatham Co, GA[156, 163]
Cause Of Death: Haemoplegia[156]

Eva Thompson and Samuel "Sam" Frazier had the following children:

    i.   Minnie Frazier (daughter of Samuel "Sam" Frazier and Eva Thompson) was born in 1881 in SC. She married ? Gillison.

    ii.   Samuel Frazier (son of Samuel "Sam" Frazier and Eva Thompson) was born in 1882 in SC.

    iii.   Robert Frazier (son of Samuel "Sam" Frazier and Eva Thompson) was born in 1884 in SC. He married Nora ?. She was born in 1889. He married Julia ?.

    iv.   Benjamin Frazier (son of Samuel "Sam" Frazier and Eva

Thompson) was born in 1889 in SC. He married Grace ?.

31.   v.   Nancy Frazier (daughter of Samuel "Sam" Frazier and Eva Thompson) was born in 1889 in Barnwell Co, SC[137]. She died after 1940 in Chatham Co?, GA. She married Joseph "Joe" Brown about 1910 in Barnwell Co?, SC, son of Joseph "Joe" Brown and Lina Glover?. He was born on July 05, 1890 in Allendale, Barnwell (Allendale) Co, SC[137, 138]. He died on December 13, 1942 in Chatham Co, GA[139]. She married ?.

     vi.   "Mamie" Frazier (daughter of Samuel "Sam" Frazier and Eva Thompson) was born in 1892 in SC.

     vii.   John W Frazier (son of Samuel "Sam" Frazier and Eva Thompson) was born in 1893 in SC.

     viii.   Helen Frazier (daughter of Samuel "Sam" Frazier and Eva Thompson) was born in 1896 in SC.

     ix.   William "Willie" Frazier (son of Samuel "Sam" Frazier and Eva Thompson) was born in 1898 in SC. He married Minnie ?. She was born in 1897.

     x.   Susan Frazier (daughter of Samuel "Sam" Frazier and Eva Thompson) was born in 1902 in SC.

Generation 7

104. **? Washington** was born in SC. He married **?**.

105. **?** was born in SC.

? and ? Washington had the following children:

52.   i.   Joseph "Joe" Washington (son of ? Washington and ?) was born about 1835 in SC. He died after 1883 in SC?. He married Tena ? about 1855 in SC, daughter of ? and ?. She was born about 1835 in SC. She died after 1883 in SC?.

     ii.   Daniel? Washington (son of ? Washington and ?) was born in 1842.

     iii.   Benjamin? Washington (son of ? Washington and ?) was born in 1846.

     iv.   D C Washington (son of ? Washington and ?) was born in 1854 in SC. He married Judy ?. She was born in 1856 in SC.

106. **?** was born in SC. He married **?**.

107. **?** was born in SC.

? and ? had the following child:

53.   i.   Tena ? (daughter of ? and ?) was born about 1835 in SC. She died after 1883 in SC?. She married Joseph "Joe" Washington about 1855 in SC, son of ? Washington and ?. He was born about 1835 in SC. He died after 1883 in SC?.

108. **? Robinson** was born in SC. He married **?**.

109. **?** was born in SC.

? and ? Robinson had the following child:

54.   i.   Robert Robinson (son of ? Robinson and ?) was born in July 1825 in SC[146, 147]. He died between 1900-1910 in SC. He married Hester ? about 1850 in Beaufort Co?, SC, daughter of ? and ?. She was born in May 1830 in SC[147]. She died between 1900-1910 in SC?.

110. **?** was born in SC. He married **?**.

111. **?** was born in SC.

? and ? had the following child:

55.   i.   Hester ? (daughter of ? and ?) was born in May 1830 in SC[147]. She died between 1900-1910 in SC?. She married Robert Robinson about 1850 in Beaufort Co?, SC, son of ? Robinson and ?. He was born in July 1825 in SC[146, 147]. He died between 1900-1910 in SC.

114. **?** was born in SC. He married **?**.

115. **?** was born in SC.

? and ? had the following child:

57.   i.   Mary ? (daughter of ? and ?) was born about 1820 in SC. She died between 1880-1900 in SC. She married Fortune Curry about 1850 in SC. He was born about 1815 in SC. He died between 1870-1880 in SC.

116. **? Alston** was born in SC. He married **?**.

117. **?** was born in SC.

? and ? Alston had the following child:

58.   i.   Benjamin "Ben" Alston (son of ? Alston and ?) was born in August 1845 in SC[148]. He died on August 15, 1918 in Savannah, Chatham Co, GA (SC)[139, 149]. He married Lucretia ? about 1863 in Beaufort Co?, SC, daughter of ? and ?. She was born about 1840 in GA (SC). She died between 1880-1900 in SC.

118. **?** was born in SC. He married **?**.

119. **?** was born in SC.

? and ? had the following child:

59.   i.   Lucretia ? (daughter of ? and ?) was born about 1840 in GA (SC). She died between 1880-1900 in SC. She married Benjamin "Ben" Alston about 1863 in Beaufort Co?, SC, son of ? Alston and ?. He was born in August 1845 in SC[148]. He died on August 15, 1918 in Savannah, Chatham Co, GA (SC)[139, 149].

120. **David? Brown**, son of Joe Brown and was born about 1854 in SC. He died between 1880-1900 in SC?. He married **Millie? Hay?** about 1870 in SC.

121. **Millie? Hay?** was born about 1852 in SC. She died between 1880-1900 in SC?.

More About David? Brown:
Census: 1870
Census: 1880

More About Millie? Hay?:
Census: 1870
Census: 1880

Notes for Millie? Hay?:
Also born GA [census]

Millie? Hay? and David? Brown had the following child:

60.   i.   Joseph "Joe" Brown (son of David? Brown and Millie? Hay?) was born in September 1871 in SC. He died between 1910-1920 in Barnwell Co?, SC. He married Lina Glover? about 1889 in Barnwell Co?, SC, daughter of ? and ?. She was born in January

1872 in SC. She died between 1910-1920 in Barnwell Co?, SC.

122. **?** was born in SC. He married **?**.

123. **?** was born in GA (SC).

? and ? had the following child:

61.   i.   Lina Glover? (daughter of ? and ?) was born in January 1872 in SC. She died between 1910-1920 in Barnwell Co?, SC. She married Joseph "Joe" Brown about 1889 in Barnwell Co?, SC, son of David? Brown and Millie? Hay?. He was born in September 1871 in SC. He died between 1910-1920 in Barnwell Co?, SC.

124. **Smart Frazier**, son of ? Frazier and ? was born about 1821 in SC. He died between 1910-1920 in SC?. He married **Minda Jones** about 1853 in Barnwell Co?, SC.

125. **Minda Jones**, daughter of ? Jones and ? was born in September 1832 in SC[164]. She died between 1900-1910 in Barnwell Co?, SC.

More About Smart Frazier:
Census: 1870 in Allendale, Barnwell (Allendale) Co, SC[158]
Occupation: Farmer[158, 159]
Census: 1880 in Allendale, Barnwell (Allendale) Co, SC[159]
Census: 1900
Census: 1910 in Allendale, Barnwell (Allendale) Co, SC[145]

More About Minda Jones:
Census: 1870 in Allendale, Barnwell (Allendale) Co, SC[158]
Occupation: Keeps house[158]
Occupation: Laborer[159]
Census: 1880 in Allendale, Barnwell (Allendale) Co, SC[159]
Occupation: Farm laborer[164]
Census: 1900 in Allendale, Barnwell (Allendale) Co, SC[164]

Minda Jones and Smart Frazier had the following children:

62.   i.   Samuel "Sam" Frazier (son of Smart Frazier and Minda Jones) was born in July 1854 in Barnwell Co?, SC[144]. He died on March 19, 1928 in Chatham Co, GA[155]. He married Eva Thompson about 1879 in Barnwell Co?, SC, daughter of Adam Thompson

and Mary ?. She was born in May 1860 in Allendale, Barnwell Co, SC[144, 156]. She died on January 25, 1929 in Mutual Quarters, Mil. 8, Chatham Co, GA[156, 157].

ii. Mary Frazier (daughter of Smart Frazier and Minda Jones) was born in 1857 in SC.

iii. Taylor Frazier (son of Smart Frazier and Minda Jones) was born in 1859 in SC. He married Minda ?. She was born in 1855 in SC.

iv. Betty Frazier (daughter of Smart Frazier and Minda Jones) was born in 1861 in SC.

v. Sidney Frazier (son of Smart Frazier and Minda Jones) was born in 1863 in SC.

vi. Nancy Frazier (daughter of Smart Frazier and Minda Jones) was born in 1865 in SC.

vii. Benjamin "Ben" Frazier (son of Smart Frazier and Minda Jones) was born in 1867 in SC. He married Martha Hay?. She was born in 1872.

viii. Tenor Frazier (daughter of Smart Frazier and Minda Jones) was born in 1874 in SC.

ix. Josephine "Josie" Frazier (daughter of Smart Frazier and Minda Jones) was born in 1879 in SC. She married William Dunbar. He was born in 1873 in SC.

x. Susan Frazier (daughter of Smart Frazier and Minda Jones) was born in 1881 in SC.

126. **Adam Thompson** was born about 1820 in SC. He died between 1870-1880 in SC. He married **Mary ?** about 1850 in SC.

127. **Mary ?** was born about 1825 in SC. She died after 1870 in SC.

More About Adam Thompson:
Occupation: Farm laborer[162]
Census: 1870 in Allendale, Barnwell Co, SC[162]

More About Mary ?:
Occupation: ? Weaver[162]
Census: 1870 in Allendale, Barnwell Co, SC[162]

Census: 1880

Mary ? and Adam Thompson had the following children:

 i. George Thompson (son of Adam Thompson and Mary ?) was born in 1854 in SC.

 ii. Maria Thompson (daughter of Adam Thompson and Mary ?) was born in 1856 in SC.

63. iii. Eva Thompson (daughter of Adam Thompson and Mary ?) was born in May 1860 in Allendale, Barnwell Co, SC[144, 156]. She died on January 25, 1929 in Mutual Quarters, Mil. 8, Chatham Co, GA[156, 157]. She married Samuel "Sam" Frazier about 1879 in Barnwell Co?, SC, son of Smart Frazier and Minda Jones. He was born in July 1854 in Barnwell Co?, SC[144]. He died on March 19, 1928 in Chatham Co, GA[155].

 iv. Ellen Thompson (daughter of Adam Thompson and Mary ?) was born in 1862 in SC.

 v. Catherine Thompson (daughter of Adam Thompson and Mary ?) was born in 1864 in SC.

 vi. Thomas Thompson (son of Adam Thompson and Mary ?) was born in 1866 in SC.

Generation 8

240. **Joe Brown** was born about 1810 in SC. He died between 1870-1880 in SC?. He married about 1850.

Joe Brown had the following child:

120. i. David? Brown (son of Joe Brown and) was born about 1854 in SC. He died between 1880-1900 in SC?. He married Millie? Hay? about 1870 in SC. She was born about 1852 in SC. She died between 1880-1900 in SC?.

248. **? Frazier** was born in SC. He married **?**.

249. **?** was born in SC.

? and ? Frazier had the following child:

124. i. Smart Frazier (son of ? Frazier and ?) was born about 1821 in SC. He died between 1910-1920 in SC?. He married Minda

Jones about 1853 in Barnwell Co?, SC, daughter of ? Jones and ?. She was born in September 1832 in SC[164]. She died between 1900-1910 in Barnwell Co?, SC.

250. **? Jones** was born in SC. He married **?**.

251. **?** was born in SC.

? and ? Jones had the following child:

125.   i.   Minda Jones (daughter of ? Jones and ?) was born in September 1832 in SC[164]. She died between 1900-1910 in Barnwell Co?, SC. She married Smart Frazier about 1853 in Barnwell Co?, SC, son of ? Frazier and ?. He was born about 1821 in SC. He died between 1910-1920 in SC?.

Sources

1   Eddie Mazo, December 1997, GA, Social Security Death Index, www.ancestry.com.

2   Eddie Mazo, Certificate of Death, #054861, Sumter, GA, State Registrar, Atlanta, GA.

3   Delored Curry death certificate.

4   Kressie Joe Curry, Birth register, no name, 2-23-1948, Vital records, Chatham Co Health Dept, PO Box 14257, Savannah, GA.

5   Eddie Mazo, December 1997, GA, Social Security Death Index, www.ancestry.com.

6   Jones household, 1920 United States Federal Census, Fulton, GA, ancestry.com & Microfilm, PA State Library, Hbg, PA.

7   Bank household, 1900 United States Census, Jefferson, AL, ancestry.com & Microfilm, PA State Library, Hbg, PA.

8   Moore household, 1940 US Federal census, Edward Mason, Atlanta, GA, anceestry.com.

9   Eddie Mazo, United States World War II Army Enlistment Records, 1938-1946, NARA, www.ancestry.com.

10   Eddie Mazo, United States WW II Army Enlistment Records, 1938-1946, NARA, www.ancestry.com.

11   Mr. Eddie Mazo, United States Dept. of the Interior, NSP, Andersonville National Historical Site, Andersonville, GA, Gerry Allen.

Sources (con't)

12   Mr. Eddie Mazo, Sect I, # 682, United States Dept. of the Interior, NSP, Andersonville National Historical Site, Andersonville, GA, Gerry Allen.

13   Delored Curry death cerrtificate, #124-544, February, 1948, Chatham, GA, State Office of Vital Records.

14   Mack Mason, Social Security numident record, application for SS-5, SSA, Nov 2006, Baltimore, MD.

15   Mack Mason death dertificate, #24230, #1271, September 1962, Chatham, GA, State Office of Vital Records.

16   Mack Mason Sr. death certificate, #24230, September 1962, Georgia Deaths 1919-98, Chatham, GA, www.ancestry.com, Kathryn Gordon Hamby.

17   Mack Mason Sr., GA Deaths, 1919-1998, #24230, www.ancestry.com.

18   Mason household, 1910 United States Census, Jefferson, GA, ancestry.com & Microfilm, PA State Library, Hbg, PA.

19   Mason-Thompson marriage, State of Georgia, Washington Co, Marriage license, Washington Co Probate Court, 1902.

20   Mason-Thompson marriage, Wash. Co Marriage Records, State of Georgia, Washington Co, Washington Co Probate Court, 1902, Book I, #519.

21   More household, 1900 United States Census, Washington Co, GA, ancestry.com & Microfilm, PA State Library, Hbg, PA.

22   Mason household, 1900 United States Census, Washington, GA, ancestry.com & Microfilm, PA State Library, Hbg, PA.

23   Mack Mason, Jeff. Co Tax Digest 1907, Office of Probate Court, Jeff. Co, Courthouse, Louisville, GA.

24   Mack Mason, Jefferson County Tax Digest 1907, Office of Probate Court, Louisville, Ga, Washington Co Hist. Society, Sandersville, PA Loretta Ceto, July 2007.

25   Mason household, 1910 United States Census, Washington, GA, ancestry.com & Microfilm, PA State Library, Hbg, PA.

26   Mason household, 1920 United States Census, Jefferson, GA, www.ancestry.com, Kathryn Gordon Hamby.

27   Mason household, 1920 United States Census, Jefferson, GA, www.ancestry.com, Kathryn Gordon Hamby.

28   Mason household, 1930 United States Census, Chatham, GA, ancestry.com & Microfilm, PA State Library, Hbg, PA.

Sources (con't)

29 Mason household, 1930 United States Census, Chatham Co, GA, ancestry.com & Microfilm, PA State Library, Hbg, PA.

30 Mason household, 1940 US Federal census, Mack Savannah, GA, anceestry.com.

31 Mack Mason, 258-34-9996, SS-5, Application for SSA Number, Baltimore, MD.

32 Mack Mason, September 1962, GA, Social Security Death Index, www.ancestry.com.

33 Shatteen household, 1900 United States Census, Washington Co, GA, ancestry.com & Microfilm, PA State Library, Hbg, PA.

34 Mason household, 1920 United States Census, Jefferson, GA, ancestry.com & Microfilm, PA State Library, Hbg, PA.

35 Mason household, 1920 United States Census, Chatham, GA, ancestry.com & Microfilm, PA State Library, Hbg, PA.

36 Forsyth-Curry marriage, Marriage License, State of GA, Chatham County, April 17, 1948. #059026, January 14, 1999, Georgia State Office of Vital Records, GA.

37 Cressie Curry, December 1998, issued PA, resided GA, Social Security Death Index, www.ancestry.com.

38 Cressie Curry death certificate, #059026, January 14, 1999, Georgia State Office of Vital Records, GA.

39 Forsyth-Curry marriage, Marriage Licnese, State of GA, Chatham County, April 17, 1948.

40 Robert Forsythe, SS-5 application, Application for SSN, Social Security Administration, 1945.

41 Robert Forsythe, Robert Forsythe, United States Veterans Cemeteries, ca. 1800-2006, Tahoma Nat'l Cemetery, NCA, Provo, UT, myfamily.com, Inc., 2006, www.ancestry.com.

42 Robert Forsythe, Social Security Death Index, Provo, UT, 259-40-7505, www.ancestry.com.

43 Forsyth-Curry marriage, Marriage License, State of GA, Chatham County, April 17, 1948.

44 Robert Forsythe, Social Security numident record, application for SS-5, SSA, Nov 2006, Baltimore, MD.

Sources (con't)

45 Dunham household, 1930 United States Census, Chatham Co, GA, ancestry.com & Microfilm, PA State Library, Hbg, PA.

46 Washington household, 1940 US Federal census, Nina Washington, Savannah, GA, anceestry.com.

47 Robert Forsythe, United States Veterans Cemeteries, ca. 1800-2006, Tahoma Nat'l Cemetery, NCA, Provo, UT, myfamily.com, Inc., 2006, www.ancestry.com.

48 Nina Washington Forsythe, death certificate, Vitals Records, Ga Dept. of Public Health, 1944, Savannah, Chatham, GA.

49 Robert Forsythe, Tahoma National Cemetery
Maple Valley, King County, Washington
18600 Southeast 240th St.
Kent, WA 98042-4868.

50 Robert Forsythe, United States Veterans Cemeteries, ca. 1800-2006, Section J, Row B, site 85, Tahoma Nat'l Cemetery, NCA, Provo, UT, myfamily.com, Inc., 2006, www.ancestry.com.

51 Curry household, 1940 US Federal census, Fred. Curry, Savannah, GA, anceestry.com.

52 Cressie Mazo, SS-5, Application for SSN, 202-40-5156, March 1966, Social Security Administration.

53 Elizabeth Curry, Certificate of Death, Custodians #1401, October 1965, Vital records, Chatham Co Health Dept, PO Box 14257, Savannah, GA.

54 Cressie Curry death certificate, #059026, January 14, 1999, Georgia State Office of Vital Records, GA and Cressie Curry, December 10, 1998, PA, Social Security Death Index, www.ancestry.com.

55 Cressie Curry, December 10, 1998, GA, Social Security Death Index, www.ancestry.com.

56 Aggie Palmer, Certificate of Death, Commonwealth of GA, Stae Board of Health, File #9966, Ivey, GA, Mar 1922.

57 Mason household, 1900 United States Census, Washington, GA, ancestry.com & Microfilm, PA State Library, Hbg, PA.

58 Mason household, 1870 United States Census, Washington, GA, ancestry.com & Microfilm, PA State Library, Hbg, PA.

59 Mason household, 1870 United States Census, Washington, GA, ancestry.com & Microfilm, PA State Library, Hbg, PA.

Sources (con't)

60 Mason household, 1880 United States Census, Washington, GA, FHL 1254171, Film T9-0171, p 360B, www.familysearch.org.

61 Mason household, 1880 United States Census, Washington, GA, ancestry.com & Microfilm, PA State Library, Hbg, PA.

62 Edward Mason, 1888, Savannah, GA Directories, 1888-91, www.ancestry.com.

63 Mason household, 1870 United States Census, Washington, GA, Roll M593 182, p 261, Image 199, ancestry.com & Microfilm, PA State Library, Hbg, PA.

64 Mason household, 1880 United States Census, Washington, GA, Roll T9-171, Film 1254171, p 360B, ED 129, Image 0102, ancestry.com & Microfilm, PA State Library, Hbg, PA.

65 Aggie Palmer, Certificate of Death, Commonwealth of GA, State Board of Health, File #9966, Ivey, GA, Mar 1922.

66 Mason-Wicker, Marriage license, State of Georgia, Washington County, Probate court, Sandersville, GA.

67 Mason-Clayton, Marriage license, State of Georgia, Washington County, Probate court, Sandersville, GA.

68 Thompson household, 1900 United States Census, Jefferson Co, GA, ancestry.com & Microfilm, PA State Library, Hbg, PA.

69 Thompson-Shatteen, marriage license, State of GA, Wahsington Co, Marriage records bk E, p 281, 1879-1885, Probate court of Washington Co, Sandersville, GA.

70 Thompson household, 1880 United States Census, Washington Co, GA, ancestry.com & Microfilm, PA State Library, Hbg, PA.

71 Shatteen household, 1880 United States Census, Washington Co, GA, ancestry.com & Microfilm, PA State Library, Hbg, PA.

72 Forsythe household, 1900 United States Census, Duval, FL, ancestry.com & Microfilm, PA State Library, Hbg, PA.

73 Percy Forsythe, Chatham County, GA Probate court, Wills, Estates, Admins, etc., F778, Adm 1942.

74 Nina Washington Forsyth, Cemetery Record, City of Savannah, Cemeteries Dept., Savannah, GA c/o Jerry Flemming, Director of Cemeteries.

75 Nina Forsythe, Chatham County, GA Probate court, Wills, Estates, Admins, etc., F806, Adm 1944.

Sources (con't)

76 Percy Campbell Forsythe, Naturalization index, NY Southern intentions, Percy Forsyth, 232663, 398, fotenote.com.

77 Forsyth household, 1910 United States Census, Duval, FL, ancestry.com & Microfilm, PA State Library, Hbg, PA.

78 Forsythe household, 1930 United States Census, Washington DC, ancestry.com & Microfilm, PA State Library, Hbg, PA.

79 Percy Campbell Forsythe, Mariners killed in WW2, City of Atlanta, www.usmm.org.

80 Percy C Forsythe, US Rosters of World War II Dead, 1939-1945, Merchant Marine, 196897, www.ancestry.com.

81 Robinson household, 1910 United States Census, Chatham Co, GA, ancestry.com & Microfilm, PA State Library, Hbg, PA.

82 Robinson household, 1920 United States Census, Chatham Co, GA, ancestry.com & Microfilm, PA State Library, Hbg, PA.

83 Freddie Curry, Certificate of Death, Custodians #1582, November 1964, Vital records, Chatham Co Health Dept, PO Box 14257, Savannah, GA.

84 Freddie Curry, Social Security numident record, application for SS-5, SSA, Nov 2006, Baltimore, MD.

85 Mack Mason, Chatham County Deaths, Wyonona Burgstiner, wburgstiner@yahoo.com.

86 Curry household, 1930 United States Census, Chatham, GA, T626, 2, 667, www.ancestry.com, GA-Census-lookup-d, Gina.

87 Curry-Brown marriage, Probate Court, Savannah, GA, p 307, bk 2R's, Sept. 17, 1928, application.

88 Elizabeth Curry, Chatham County Deaths, Wyonona Burgstiner, wburgstiner@yahoo.com.

89 No name Curry, Birth register, Dept. of Public Health, Chatam Co, GA, 2/15/07, Dunkin Curria & Betsy.

90 Curry household, United States Census, 1910, Chatham, GA, ancestry.com & Microfilm, PA State Library, Hbg, PA.

91 Curry household, United States Census, 1920, Chatham, GA, ancestry.com & Microfilm, PA State Library, Hbg, PA.

92 Curry household, 1930 United States Census, Chatham, GA, ancestry.com & Microfilm, PA State Library, Hbg, PA.

Sources (con't)

93 Curry household, 1930 United States Census, Chatham, GA, T626, 2, 667, ancestry.com & Microfilm, PA State Library, Hbg, PA.

94 Freddie Curry, Lot 60, Sec B, Cemetery Record, City of Savannah, Cemeteries Dept., Savannah, GA c/o Jerry Flemming, Director of Cemeteries.

95 Brown household, 1920 United States Census, Allendale Co, GA, ancestry.com & Microfilm, PA State Library, Hbg, PA.

96 Mrs. Elizabeth Curry, Savannah Morning News, Oct 17, 1965, Wyonona Burgstiner, wburgstiner@yahoo.com.

97 Elizabeth Curry, Lot 60, Sec B, Cemetery Record, City of Savannah, Cemeteries Dept., Savannah, GA c/o Jerry Flemming, Director of Cemeteries.

98 Neal household, 1880 United States Census, Washington, GA, ancestry.com & Microfilm, PA State Library, Hbg, PA.

99 Mason-Walker, Marriage license, State of Georgia, Washington County, Probate court, Sandersville, GA.

100 Mason-Adams, Marriage license, State of Georgia, Washington County, Probate court, Sandersville, GA.

101 Mason-Andrews, Marriage license, State of Georgia, Washington County, Probate court, Sandersville, GA.

102 Mason-Moffett, Marriage license, State of Georgia, Washington County, Probate court, Sandersville, GA.

103 Mason-Cumming, Marriage license, State of Georgia, Washington County, Probate court, Sandersville, GA.

104 Brown household, 1870 United States Census, Washington Co, GA, ancestry.com & Microfilm, PA State Library, Hbg, PA.

105 Thompson household, 1870 United States Census, Chatham Co, GA, ancestry.com & Microfilm, PA State Library, Hbg, PA.

106 Thomson household, 1880 US Federal Census, SD 3, ED 36, pg 11, Chatham, GA, p732, www.ancestry.com.

107 Thompson-Mason, Marriage license, State of Georgia, Washington County, Probate court, Sandersville, GA.

108 Thompson-Key, Marriage license, State of Georgia, Washington County, Probate court, Sandersville, GA.

Sources (con't)

109 Sallie Shateen, Cert of Death, File #26470, Reg.#1516, 11/10/1927, GA
     Virtual Vault, http://content.sos.state.ga.us/cdm4/gadeaths.php.

110 Sallie Shateen, Georgia Deaths, 1919-98, Chatham Co, GA, 1927,
     www.ancestry.com.

111 Shattine household, 1910 United States Census, Jefferson Co, GA,
     ancestry.com & Microfilm, PA State Library, Hbg, PA.

112 Shatteen household, 1920 United States Census, Chatham Co, GA,
     ancestry.com & Microfilm, PA State Library, Hbg, PA.

113 Shatteen-Hall, Marriage license, State of Georgia, Washington County,
     Probate court, Sandersville, GA.

114 Theophilus Forsythe, Cert of Death, File #05483, Reg.#130, 5/23/1919, GA
     Virtual Vault, http://content.sos.state.ga.us/cdm4/gadeaths.php.

115 Washington household, 1900 United States Census, Beaufort Co, SC,
     ancestry.com & Microfilm, PA State Library, Hbg, PA.

116 Joe Washington Jr., certificate of death, Beaufort, SC, 1922, South Carolina
     DHEC, Columbia, SC.

117 Robinson household, 1910 United States Census, Chatham, GA,
     ancestry.com & Microfilm, PA State Library, Hbg, PA.

118 Mary Washington, death record, Georgia Deaths, 1919-98, #7748,
     www.ancestry.com.

119 Washington (DC) household, 1880 United States Census, Beaufort Co, SC,
     www,ancestry.com.

120 Washington (Tennia) household, 1880 United States Census, Beaufort Co,
     SC, www,ancestry.com.

121 Washington household, 1900 United States Census, Beaufort Co, SC,
     www,ancestry.com.

122 Washington household, 1910 United States Census, Beaufort Co, SC,
     www,ancestry.com.

123 Robinson household, 1880 United States Census, Beaufort Co, SC,
     ancestry.com & Microfilm, PA State Library, Hbg, PA.

124 Robinson household, 1920 United States Census, Chatham, GA,
     ancestry.com & Microfilm, PA State Library, Hbg, PA.

125 Dunham household, 1930 United States Census, Chatham, GA,
     ancestry.com & Microfilm, PA State Library, Hbg, PA.

Sources (con't)

126   Mary Washington, Laurel Grove Cemetery, Jerry Flemming, Director of Cemeteries, Savannah, GA.

127   Curry household, 1900 United States Census, Chatham, GA, ancestry.com & Microfilm, PA State Library, Hbg, PA.

128   Rosa Louise Curry, Certificate of Death, Commonwealth of GA, Stae Board of Health, File #13727, Chatham, GA, June 1922.

129   Henry Curry, Chatham County Deaths, Wyonona Burgstiner, wburgstiner@yahoo.com.

130   Duncan Curry, Death Register, June 1914, Chatham County Health Dept., Savannah, GA.

131   Curry household, United States Census, 1870, Beaufort Co, SC, ancestry.com & Microfilm, PA State Library, Hbg, PA.

132   Curry household, United States Census, 1880, Hampton, SC, ancestry.com & Microfilm, PA State Library, Hbg, PA.

133   Duncan Curry, Savannah, GA Directories, 1888-91, Provo, UT, myfamily.com, Inc., 2001, www.ancestry.com.

134   Colored boy, Birth Certificate, January 1909, Vital records, Chatham Co Health Dept, PO Box 14257, Savannah, GA.

135   Duncan Curry, death certificate, Chatham, GA, Physician's Certificate of the Cause of death, June 1914, CCHD, Savannah, GA.

136   Alston household, 1880 United States Census, Hampton, SC, ancestry.com & Microfilm, PA State Library, Hbg, PA.

137   Colored boy, birth certificate, April 1908, Chatham County Health Dept, Savannah, GA.

138   Joe Brown, U.S. World War 1 Draft Registration Cards, No 209, 39-1-3, A, Allendale, SC, 1942, www.ancestry.com.

139   Ben Alston, Georgia Deaths, 1919-98, Chatham, GA, Aug 1918, ancestry.com.

140   Brown household, 1900 United States Census, Barnwell Co, GA, ancestry.com & Microfilm, PA State Library, Hbg, PA.

141   Brown household, 1910 United States Census, Barnwell Co, GA, ancestry.com & Microfilm, PA State Library, Hbg, PA.

142   Brown household, United States Census, 1930, Chatham, GA, ancestry.com & Microfilm, PA State Library, Hbg, PA.

Sources (con't)

143   Brown household, 1940 US Federal census, Joe Brown, Savannah, GA, anceestry.com.

144   Frazier household, 1900 United States Census, Barnwell Co, GA, ancestry.com & Microfilm, PA State Library, Hbg, PA.

145   Frazier household, 1910 United States Census, Barnwell Co, GA, ancestry.com & Microfilm, PA State Library, Hbg, PA.

146   Robinson household, 1870 United States Census, Beaufort Co, SC, ancestry.com & Microfilm, PA State Library, Hbg, PA.

147   Robinson household, 1900 United States Census, Charleston, SC, www.amcestry.com.

148   Alston household, 1900 United States Census, Chatham, GA, www.amcestry.com.

149   Ben Alston, Laurel Grove Cem listing, Jerry Flemming, Director of Cemetery, Savannah, GA, Jerry_Flemming@SavannahGa.Gov.

150   Allston household, 1870 United States Census, Beaufort Co, SC, ancestry.com & Microfilm, PA State Library, Hbg, PA.

151   Alston household, 1880 United States Census, Beaufort Co, SC, ancestry.com & Microfilm, PA State Library, Hbg, PA.

152   Benjamin Alston, Savannah, GA Directories, 1888-91, Provo, UT, myfamily.com, Inc., 2001, www.ancestry.com.

153   Alston household, 1910 United States Census, Chatham, GA, ancestry.com & Microfilm, PA State Library, Hbg, PA.

154   Alston household, 1880 United States Census, Lawnton, SC, ancestry.com & Microfilm, PA State Library, Hbg, PA.

155   Samuel Frazier, Georgia Deaths, 1919-1998, ancestry.com.

156   Eva Frazier, Certificate of Death,January 1929, Chatham County Health Dept, State file #2, Savannah, GA.

157   Eva Frazier, Georgia Deaths, 1919-1998, ancestry.com.

158   Fraisier household, 1870 United States Census, Barnwell Co, GA, ancestry.com & Microfilm, PA State Library, Hbg, PA.

159   Fraser household, 1880 United States Census, Barnwell Co, GA, ancestry.com & Microfilm, PA State Library, Hbg, PA.

160   Frazier household, 1920 United States Census, Allendale Co, GA, ancestry.com & Microfilm, PA State Library, Hbg, PA.

Sources (con't)

161   Sam Frazier, death certificate, Chatham, GA, Local registrar's record of death, March 1928, CCHD, Savannah, GA.

162   Thompson household, 1870 United States Census, Barnwell Co, GA, ancestry.com & Microfilm, PA State Library, Hbg, PA.

163   Eva Frazier, Cemetery Record, City of Savannah, Cemeteries Dept., Savannah, GA c/o Jerry Flemming, Director of Cemeteries.

164   Dunbar household, 1900 United States Census, Barnwell Co, SC, ancestry.com & Microfilm, PA State Library, Hbg, PA.

Chapter Two

Our family's photos.

Some photographs of our family.
A picture tells a thousand words.

Photo Album for Melvalean Curry

Melvalean Curry

Birth:	January 15, 1967	Father:	Ned "Eddie" Mazo
Death:	May 29, 2008	Mother:	Delores Ann Curry
Marriage:	November 21, 2001	Spouse:	Living Thompson

Marc & Mel
Thompson

Marc, Sophia &
Mel Thompson

Photo Album for Delores Ann Curry

Delores Ann Curry

Birth:	February 24, 1948	Father:	Robert J Washington Forsythe
Death:	December 16, 2000	Mother:	Lucretia "Cressie" Jo Curry
Marriage:		Spouse:	Ned "Eddie" Mazo

Delores Curry

Delores Curry

Delores Curry

Chapter Three

Our family's places.

Where we're from, born, raised, lived and roamed through.

Place Usage Report

? Monroe Funeral Home, 611 W. Broad (now MLK Jr Blvd), Savannah, Chatham Co, GA

Thompson, Eva

? Rhodes Rd., Savannah, GA

Mason, Mack

?61 Indian St., Savannah, GA

Forsythe, Robert J Washington

1108 Rogers St., Savannah, Chatham Co, GA

Brown, Elizabeth

1108 Rogers Street, Newtown, GA

Curry, Frederick "Freddie"

1109 Richard St., Savannah, Chatham Co, GA

Mason, Mack

120 Randolph St., Savannah, GA

Forsythe, Robert J Washington

Robinson, Mary

Washington, Nina

120 Reynolds St., Savannah, Chatham Co, GA

Robinson, Mary

124 Reynolds St.

Forsythe, Robert J Washington

1314 Egmond St, Brook?, Glynn Co, GA

Forsythe, Theodore (Theopolis)

1350 Augusta Rd., Savannah, Chatham Co, GA

Mason, Mack

142 Lathrope (Oglethorpe) Ave., Savannah, GA

Brown, Joseph "Joe"

143 Lathorp Ave, Savannah, GA

Brown, Elizabeth

Curry, Frederick "Freddie"

143 Lathrope (Oglethorpe) Ave., Savannah, GA

Curry, Frederick "Freddie"

145 Lathorp Ave, Savannah, GA

Mason, Mack

Thompson, Sarah "Sallie" A Shalteen

145 Lathorpe (Oglethorpe) Ave., Savannah, GA

145 Lathorpe (Oglethorpe) Ave., Savannah, GA (con't)
Mason, Mack

16 Lathrope Ave., Mutual Quarters, Chatham Co, GA
Frazier, Samuel "Sam"

1936 Dennie St., Philadelphia, PA
Curry, Lucretia "Cressie" Jo

1st Militia, Chatham Co, GA
Alston, Elizabeth "Bessie"
Curry, Duncan C

200 Broughton, Savannah, Chatham Co, GA
Mason, Edward "Ned"

2231 5th Ave., Birmingham, AL
Mazo, Ned "Eddie"

225 Hospital Drive, Plains, Sumter, GA
Mazo, Ned "Eddie"

3 E. Broad, Savannah, Chatham Co, GA
Robinson, Mary

321 Bay St., Savannah, Chatham Co, GA
Robinson, Mary
Washington, Nina

413 59th St., Washington DC
Forsythe, Percy Campbell

413/913 59th St., Washington DC
?, Margaret
Forsythe, Percy Campbell

440 Eagle St., Savannah, Chatham Co, GA
Morgan, Sallie

6 Dermon? St., Savannah, Chatham Co, GA
Alston, Elizabeth "Bessie"

6 W. Exley St., Newtown, Savannah, GA
Mason, Mack

610 Oglethorpe Ave, Savannah, GA
Curry, Duncan C

610 W. Williams St., Savannah, Chatham Co, GA
Curry, Duncan C

619 W Lumber St., Savannah, Chatham Co, GA
Curry, Duncan C

933 Odessa St., Jacksonville, FL
Forsythe, Percy Campbell

933 Odessa St., Jacksonville, FL (con't)

Forsythe, Theodore (Theopolis)

Air Corps, MOH (Hawaii)

Mazo, Ned "Eddie"

Allendale, Allendale Co, SC

Brown, Elizabeth

Brown, Joseph "Joe"

Frazier, Nancy

Allendale, Barnwell (Allendale) Co, SC

Brown, Joseph "Joe"

Brown, Joseph "Joe"

Frazier, Smart

Jones, Minda

Allendale, Barnwell (Allendale), SC

Brown, Elizabeth

Brown, Joseph "Joe"

Frazier, Nancy

Frazier, Samuel "Sam"

Glover?, Lina

Thompson, Eva

Allendale, Barnwell Co, SC

?, Mary

Thompson, Adam

Thompson, Eva

Anderson Nat'l Cemetery, Andersonville, Macon, GA

Mazo, Ned "Eddie"

Atlanta, Fulton Co, GA

Brown, Ella Lee

Atlanta, Fulton, GA

Mazo, Ned "Eddie"

Augusta Rd., Chatham Co, GA

Thompson, Sarah "Sallie" A Shalteen

Bahamas, West Indies (Eng)

Forsythe, Percy Campbell

Baldoc, Allendale Co Co, SC

Thompson, Eva

Baldoc, Allendale Co, SC

Frazier, Samuel "Sam"

Barnwell Co, SC

Barnwell Co, SC (con't)

Frazier, Nancy

Barnwell Co?, SC

Brown, Joseph "Joe"

Brown, Joseph "Joe"

Frazier, Nancy

Frazier, Samuel "Sam"

Frazier, Smart

Glover?, Lina

Jones, Minda

Thompson, Eva

Batow 85th Dt., Jefferson Co, GA

Mason, Mack

bds ss Indian Ln, 3d E. of canal, Savannah, Chatham Co, GA

Alston, Benjamin "Ben"

Curry, Duncan C

Beaufort Co?, SC

?, Hester

?, Lucretia

Alston, Benjamin "Ben"

Alston, Elizabeth "Bessie"

Curry, Duncan C

Robinson, Mary

Robinson, Robert

Washington, Joseph "Joe"

Beaufort, Beaufort Co, SC

Robinson, Mary

Washington, Joseph "Joe"

Bill Exley farm, SC

Brown, Joseph "Joe"

Birmingham, Jefferson, AL

Mazo, Ned "Eddie"

Brunswick, Glynn Co, GA

Forsythe, Theodore (Theopolis)

Bull Pond, Barnwell (Allendale), SC

Frazier, Samuel "Sam"

Thompson, Eva

Bull Pond, Barnwell Co, SC

Frazier, Nancy

Cato, Washington, GA
  ?, Hannah
  Mason, Alfred
Charity Hospital, Savannah, Chatham Co, GA
  Washington, Nina
Chatham Co, GA
  Brown, Elizabeth
  Brown, Joseph "Joe"
  Forsythe, Percy Campbell
  Frazier, Samuel "Sam"
  Washington, Nina
Chatham Co, GA?
  ?, Nancy
  Thompson, Stephen
Chatham Co?, GA
  Alston, Elizabeth "Bessie"
  Frazier, Nancy
Chestnut Hill, Philadelphia, PA
  Curry, Delores Ann
Church St., Savannah, Chatham Co, GA
  Morgan, Sallie
Daufuskie, Beaufort Co, SC
  Forsythe, Robert J Washington
  Washington, Joseph "Joe"
  Washington, Nina
Daughter Annie's Home, Savannah, Chatham Co, GA
  Mason, Mack
Davisboro, Washingtion Co, GA
  Morgan, Thomas
Davisboro, Washington Co, GA
  ?, May A
  Brown, George
  Morgan, Sallie
  Shatteen, Anne
  Shatteen, Mason
  Thompson, Peter
  Thompson, Sarah "Sallie" A Shalteen
Davisboro, Washington, GA
  Brown, Ranie

Davisboro, Washington, GA (con't)
Mason, Edward "Ned"
Mason, Mack
Delray Beach, Palm Beach Co., FL
Curry, Melvalean
Dillsburg, York Co, PA
Thompson, Living
District 8, Chatham Co, GA
Brown, Elizabeth
Brown, Joseph "Joe"
Curry, Frederick "Freddie"
Frazier, Nancy
Thompson, Sarah "Sallie" A Shalteen
District 8, Chatham Co, GA (Mary)
Mason, Mack
Dorchester Funeral Home, Midway, Liberty Co, GA
Curry, Lucretia "Cressie" Jo
Dt 5, Savannah, Chatham Co, GA
?, Nancy
Thompson, Stephen
Dt 8, Chatham Co, GA
Thompson, Stephen
Edisto Island, Charleston Co, SC
?, Hester
Robinson, Robert
Farm laborer
Morgan, Sallie
GA
?
?
?
?
?
?
?
?
?
?, Hannah
?, Hilda

GA (con't)

?, Lavinia

?, Lucretia

?, Lula "Lou"

?, May A

?, Nellie

Adams, Ellen

Alston, Elizabeth "Bessie"

Brown, George

Brown, Maria

Brown, Mary

Brown, Rachel

Brown, Remus

Brown, Samuel

Brown, Simon

Curry, Charles "Charlie"

Curry, Delores Ann

Curry, Duncan C

Curry, Edmonia

Curry, Elizabeth "Bessie"

Curry, Frampton

Curry, Frank

Curry, Frederick "Fred"

Curry, Hilda

Curry, Ira

Curry, Leola

Curry, Nancy

Curry, Samuel

Curry, Solomon

Curry, William

Curry, William "Willie"

Forsythe, Nina

Mason, "Maggie"

Mason, Addie

Mason, Alfred

Mason, Alfred

Mason, Alonzo

Mason, Andrew

Mason, Anne "Annie"

GA (con't)

Mason, Anne Lee
Mason, Austin
Mason, Benjamin
Mason, Bessie
Mason, Cleveland
Mason, Daniel
Mason, Dicey
Mason, Eddie
Mason, Ella
Mason, George
Mason, George
Mason, George W
Mason, Jacob "Jake"
Mason, James
Mason, James?
Mason, Jane
Mason, Janice
Mason, Jefferson D
Mason, Jesse
Mason, John Dooly
Mason, Josephine
Mason, Linda
Mason, Mack
Mason, Maria
Mason, Mollie
Mason, Moses?
Mason, Noah
Mason, Oliver
Mason, Plum
Mason, Reuben
Mason, Robert B
Mason, Thomas
Mason, Thomas
Mason, Willard
Mason, Willis
Mazo, Ned "Eddie"
Middleton, Daniel
Morgan, Sallie

GA (con't)

Robinson, Thomas J

Shateen, ?

Shatteen, Isaac

Shatteen, James

Shatteen, Jesse

Shatteen, Lillie

Shatteen, Linnie

Shatteen, Mason

Thompson, " Abbie"

Thompson, Cato C

Thompson, Cornelius

Thompson, Henry

Thompson, J J

Thompson, Joshua A

Thompson, Julia

Thompson, Larfield

Thompson, Layer

Thompson, Lornie

Thompson, Samuel?

Thompson, Seymour

Thompson, Stephen

Thompson, Susan

Walker, Pheobe

Washington, Charles H Robinson

GA?

?, Nancy

Forsythe, Mildred

Forsythe, Percy Campbell

Morgan, Thomas

Shatteen, Anne

Shatteen, Mason

Thompson, Peter

Thompson, Stephen

Washington, Nina

Grange, Jefferson Co, GA

Thompson, Peter

Gray's Hill, Beaufort Co, SC

Washington, Joseph "Joe"

Green Mount Cemetery, Philadelphia, Philadelphia Co, PA

Curry, Delores Ann

Greenwood Cemetery

Forsythe, Theodore (Theopolis)

Harrisburg, Dauphin Co, PA

Thompson, Living

Hilton Head, Beaufort Co, SC

?, Hester

Robinson, Mary

Robinson, Robert

Ivey, Johnson Co, GA

Mason, Aggie

Jacksonville, Duval Co, FL

?, Margaret

Curry, Frederick "Fred"

Forsythe, Percy Campbell

Forsythe, Theodore (Theopolis)

Jefferson Co, GA

Mason, Mack

Mazo, Ned "Eddie"

Thompson, Peter

Jefferson, Philadelphia Co, PA

Curry, Melvalean

John Boyd, 1412 Alberry? St, GA

Forsythe, Theodore (Theopolis)

Johnson Landry Rd., Allendale Co, SC

Brown, Joseph "Joe"

Laurel Grove Cemetery, Savannah, Chatham Co, GA

Brown, Elizabeth

Curry, Duncan C

Curry, Frederick "Freddie"

Frazier, Samuel "Sam"

Morgan, Sallie

Thompson, Eva

Washington, Nina

Laurel Grove South Cemetery, Savannah, Chatham Co, GA

Robinson, Mary

Lawnton, Hampton Co, SC

?, Mary

Lawnton, Hampton Co, SC (con't)
Alston, Elizabeth "Bessie"
Curry, Duncan C
Lawnton, Hampton, SC
?, Lucretia
Alston, Benjamin "Ben"
Liberty Regional Medical Center, Hinesville, Liberty Co, GA
Curry, Lucretia "Cressie" Jo
Lincoln Cemetery, Chatham Co, GA
Thompson, Sarah "Sallie" A Shalteen
Louisville, Jefferson Co, GA
Mason, Mack
Thompson, Sarah "Sallie" A Shalteen
McKelsey-Powell Co, 712 W Broad St., Savannah, Chatham Co, GA
Morgan, Sallie
Media, Delaware Co, PA
Curry, Melvalean
Thompson, Living
Midway Cong. Cemetery, Midway, Liberty Co, GA
Curry, Lucretia "Cressie" Jo
Midway, Liberty, GA
Curry, Lucretia "Cressie" Jo
Militia Dt 8, Chatham, GA
Alston, Benjamin "Ben"
Militia Dt 85, Jefferson Co, GA
Morgan, Sallie
Monroe Funeral Home, 611 W. Broad (now MLK Jr Blvd), Savannah, Chatham Co, GA
Thompson, Sarah "Sallie" A Shalteen
Mutual Quarters, Mil. 8, Chatham Co, GA
Thompson, Eva
Nassau, Bahamas, West Indies (Eng)
Forsythe, Nelson
NC
?, Nancy
Oak Grove Cemetery, Savannah, Chatham Co, GA
Mason, Mack
Oglethorpe Funeral Chapel, Inc., 607 Kaigler St, POB 8, Ogelthorpe, GA 31068

Oglethorpe Funeral Chapel, Inc., 607 Kaigler St, POB 8, Ogelthorpe, GA 31068 (con't)

Mazo, Ned "Eddie"

PA

Williams, Emery Ardel

Williams, Living

Williams, Living

Williams, Living

Williams, Living

Williams, Living

Williams, Living

Williams, Living

Palm Beach, Florida, USA

Thompson, Living

Pippins St., Jacksonville, FL

Forsythe, Percy Campbell

Forsythe, Theodore (Theopolis)

Plains, Sumter, GA

Mazo, Ned "Eddie"

Road from Wadley to Pressluck?, Jefferson, GA

Mason, Mack

Savannah, Chatham Co, GA

Alston, Benjamin "Ben"

Alston, Elizabeth "Bessie"

Brown, Elizabeth

Brown, Eva Mae

Brown, Joseph "Joe"

Curry, Charles "Charlie"

Curry, Delores Ann

Curry, Duncan C

Curry, Frederick "Freddie"

Curry, Lucretia "Cressie" Jo

Curry, Rosa Louise

Forsythe, Percy Campbell

Forsythe, Robert J Washington

Frazier, Nancy

Mason, Mack

Mazo, Ned "Eddie"

Morgan, Sallie

Savannah, Chatham Co, GA (con't)

Robinson, Mary

Washington, Nina

SC

?

?

?

?

?

?

?

?

?

?

?

?

?

?

?, Anna

?, Flora

?, Hester

?, Judy

?, Lucretia

?, Mary

?, Mary

?, Minda

?, Tena

Alston, ?

Alston, Albert

Alston, Benjamin "Ben"

Alston, Lucy

Alston, Mary

Brown, Adam

Brown, Benjamin

Brown, Christopher Columbus

Brown, David?

Brown, Dorothy Mae

Brown, Ella Lee

Brown, Ellis

SC (con't)

Brown, Eva Mae
Brown, James
Brown, Joe
Brown, Joseph "Joe"
Brown, Josephine
Brown, Lillian "Lillie"
Brown, Linton
Brown, Richard
Brown, William
Curry, Cyrus
Curry, Emma
Curry, Fortune
Curry, Gabriel
Curry, Pleasant
Curry, Thomas
Dunbar, ?
Dunbar, William
Dunbar, William
Frazier, "Mamie"
Frazier, ?
Frazier, Benjamin
Frazier, Benjamin "Ben"
Frazier, Betty
Frazier, Butler
Frazier, Helen
Frazier, Henry
Frazier, John W
Frazier, Josephine "Josie"
Frazier, Mary
Frazier, Minnie
Frazier, Nancy
Frazier, Robert
Frazier, Samuel
Frazier, Sidney
Frazier, Smart
Frazier, Susan
Frazier, Susan
Frazier, Taylor

SC (con't)

Frazier, Tenor
Frazier, William "Willie"
Glover?, Lina
Hay?, Millie?
Jones, ?
Jones, Minda
Robinson, ?
Robinson, Anna
Robinson, Dolly
Robinson, Elizabeth
Robinson, Emma
Robinson, John
Robinson, Joseph
Robinson, Robert
Robinson, Willis
Thompson, Adam
Thompson, Catherine
Thompson, Daniel?
Thompson, Ellen
Thompson, George
Thompson, Maria
Thompson, Stephen
Thompson, Thomas
Thompson, Thomas?
Washington, ?
Washington, ?
Washington, Aaron
Washington, Albert Ernest Robinson
Washington, D C
Washington, Dara
Washington, Elizabeth "Betsy"
Washington, Essie
Washington, George
Washington, Harold
Washington, Hasilar Neter
Washington, Joseph
Washington, Joseph "Joe"
Washington, Joseph "Joe"

SC (con't)

Washington, Lottie
Washington, Rose
Washington, Samuel
Washington, Smart
Washington, Solomon
Washington, Susan
Washington, William
Washington, William "Billie"

SC?

?, Hester
?, Tena
Brown, David?
Brown, Joe
Frazier, Smart
Hay?, Millie?
Washington, Joseph "Joe"

Seattle, King Co, WA

Forsythe, Robert J Washington

Sidney A Jones Funeral Home, 124 West Park Avenue, Savannah, Chatham Co, GA

Brown, Elizabeth

Sidney A Jones, 511 West Waldburg St., Savannah, Chatham Co, GA

Curry, Frederick "Freddie"

Springfield Plantation, Chatham Co, GA

Washington, Nina

St Peters, Beaufort Co, SC

?, Mary
Curry, Duncan C
Curry, Fortune

St. Helena Island, Beaurfort Co, SC

?, Tena
Washington, Joseph "Joe"

St. Lukes, Beaufort Co, SC

?, Hester
Robinson, Robert

St. Peters, Beaufort Co, SC

?, Lucretia
Alston, Benjamin "Ben"

Sumter Regional Hospital, Americus, Sumter Co, GA

Mazo, Ned "Eddie"

Tahoma National Cemetery, St. Kent, King Co, WA

Forsythe, Robert J Washington

Tampa, Hillsborough Co, FL

Forsythe, Nina

VA

?, Stella

Wadley, Jefferson Co, GA

Mason, Melvin

Thompson, Sarah "Sallie" A Shalteen

Wadley, Jefferson, GA

Mason, Mack

Walterboro, Colleton Co, SC

Washington, Harold

Washington Co, GA

Brown, Ranie

Mason, Aggie

Mason, Edward "Ned"

Mason, Mack

Shatteen, Anne

Thompson, Peter

Thompson, Sarah "Sallie" A Shalteen

Washington Co?, GA

?, Hannah

Brown, Ranie

Mason, Alfred

Mason, Edward "Ned"

Washington DC

?, Margaret

Forsythe, Percy Campbell

West Indies (Eng)

?

?

?, Margaret

Forsythe, Frederick

Forsythe, Hattie

Forsythe, Theodore

Forsythe, Theodore (Theopolis)

West Indies (Eng) (con't)

Hapton, Elizabeth

West Indies to Florida

Forsythe, Percy Campbell

Forsythe, Theodore (Theopolis)

Williams & Williams Funeral Home, 1012 East Gwinnett St., GA

Mason, Mack

Chapter Four

Our family's kinship.

How we are all related to one another, from present to distant past.

Kinship

Name:	Birth Date:	Relationship:
?		Husband of half sister of wife of husband
?		Husband of 2nd great grandmother of wife of husband
?		Wife of father-in-law of husband
?		Husband of half sister of wife of husband
?		Half nephew of wife of husband
?		Husband of half sister of wife of husband
?		Wife of half brother of wife of husband
?		Husband of wife of father-in-law of husband
?		3rd great grandmother of wife of husband
?		3rd great grandmother of wife of husband
?		4th great grandmother of wife of husband
?		3rd great grandfather of wife of husband
?		5th great grandmother of wife of husband
?		4th great grandmother of wife of husband
?		4th great grandmother of wife of husband
?		3rd great grandmother of wife of husband
?		3rd great grandmother of wife of husband

Name:	Birth Date:	Relationship:
?		5th great grandmother of wife of husband
?		4th great grandmother of wife of husband
?		4th great grandfather of wife of husband
?		4th great grandmother of wife of husband
?		4th great grandmother of wife of husband
?		4th great grandfather of wife of husband
?		3rd great grandfather of wife of husband
?		4th great grandmother of wife of husband
?		4th great grandfather of wife of husband
?		3rd great grandmother of wife of husband
?		4th great grandfather of wife of husband
?		3rd great grandmother of wife of husband
?		3rd great grandfather of wife of husband
?		4th great grandmother of wife of husband
?		4th great grandfather of wife of husband
?	Abt. 1820	3rd great grandmother of wife of husband
?, Anna	1883	Wife of 2nd great grand uncle of wife of husband

Name:	Birth Date:	Relationship:
?, Anne	1907	Wife of 1st great grand uncle of wife of husband
?, Flora	Abt. 1879	Wife of 2nd great grandfather of wife of husband
?, Grace		Wife of 2nd great grand uncle of wife of husband
?, Hannah	1829	2nd great grandmother of wife of husband
?, Hester	May 1830	3rd great grandmother of wife of husband
?, Hilda	1870	Wife of grand uncle of wife of husband
?, Judy	1856	Wife of 3rd great grand uncle of wife of husband
?, Julia		Wife of 2nd great grand uncle of wife of husband
?, Julia	1910	Wife of 1st cousin 4x removed of wife of husband
?, Lavinia	1866	Wife of grand uncle of wife of husband
?, Lucretia	Abt. 1840	3rd great grandmother of wife of husband
?, Lucy		Wife of 3rd great grand uncle of wife of husband
?, Lula "Lou"	1872	Wife of 1st great grand uncle of wife of husband
?, Mabel	1903	Wife of 1st cousin 4x removed of wife of husband
?, Margaret	Bet. January 1865–1870	2nd great grandmother of wife of husband
?, Mary	Abt. 1820	3rd great grandmother of wife of husband
?, Mary	Abt. 1825	4th great grandmother of wife of husband

Name:	Birth Date:	Relationship:
?, May A	Abt. 1836	2nd great grandmother of wife of husband
?, Minda	1855	Wife of 3rd great grand uncle of wife of husband
?, Minnie	1897	Wife of 2nd great grand uncle of wife of husband
?, Nancy	Abt. 1841	2nd great grandmother of wife of husband
?, Nellie	1894	Wife of 1st great grand uncle of wife of husband
?, Nora	1889	Wife of 2nd great grand uncle of wife of husband
?, Rhinor?	Abt. 1800	3rd great grandmother of wife of husband
?, Stella	1885	Wife of 1st great grand uncle of wife of husband
?, Tena	Abt. 1835	3rd great grandmother of wife of husband
Adams, Ellen	1859	Wife of 1st great grand uncle of wife of husband
Alston, ?		4th great grandfather of wife of husband
Alston, Albert	1874	2nd great grand uncle of wife of husband
Alston, Benjamin "Ben"	August 1845	3rd great grandfather of wife of husband
Alston, Elizabeth "Bessie"	December 1870	2nd great grandmother of wife of husband
Alston, Lucy	1865	2nd great grand aunt of wife of husband
Alston, Mary	1878	2nd great grand aunt of wife of husband
Andrews, Charlotte		Wife of 1st great grand uncle of wife of husband

Name:	Birth Date:	Relationship:
Brown, Adam	1924	1st great grand uncle of wife of husband
Brown, Benjamin	1919	1st great grand uncle of wife of husband
Brown, Christopher Columbus	1916	1st great grand uncle of wife of husband
Brown, David?	Abt. 1854	4th great grandfather of wife of husband
Brown, Dorothy Mae	Abt. 1920	1st great grand aunt of wife of husband
Brown, Elizabeth	Bet. 06–June 11, 1911	Great grandmother of wife of husband
Brown, Ella Lee	October 27, 1921	1st great grand aunt of wife of husband
Brown, Ellis	Abt. 1920	1st great grand uncle of wife of husband
Brown, Eva Mae	May 14, 1924	1st great grand aunt of wife of husband
Brown, George	Abt. 1822	2nd great grandfather of wife of husband
Brown, James	1880	Husband of 1st cousin 1x removed of wife of husband
Brown, Joe	Abt. 1810	5th great grandfather of wife of husband
Brown, Joseph "Joe"	September 1871	3rd great grandfather of wife of husband
Brown, Joseph "Joe"	July 05, 1890	2nd great grandfather of wife of husband
Brown, Josephine	1915	1st great grand aunt of wife of husband
Brown, Lillian "Lillie"	Abt. 1920	1st great grand aunt of wife of husband
Brown, Linton	1889	2nd great grand uncle of wife of husband
Brown, Maria	1913	2nd cousin of wife of husband
Brown, Mary	1861	1st great grand aunt of wife of husband
Brown, Rachel	1854	1st great grand aunt of wife of husband
Brown, Ranie	December 1852	Great grandmother of wife of husband

Name:	Birth Date:	Relationship:
Brown, Remus	1863	1st great grand uncle of wife of husband
Brown, Richard	1896	2nd great grand uncle of wife of husband
Brown, Samuel	1856	1st great grand uncle of wife of husband
Brown, Samuel?	Abt. 1800	3rd great grandfather of wife of husband
Brown, Simon	1857	1st great grand uncle of wife of husband
Brown, William	1892	2nd great grand uncle of wife of husband
Chapman, Mary		Wife of 1st great grand uncle of wife of husband
Clayton, Martha Ann	Abt. 1880	Wife of grand uncle of wife of husband
Cumming, Harriet		Wife of 1st great grand uncle of wife of husband
Cumming, Henry		Husband of 1st cousin 2x removed of wife of husband
Curry, Charles "Charlie"	February 08, 1912	1st great grand uncle of wife of husband
Curry, Cyrus	1859	2nd great grand uncle of wife of husband
Curry, Delores Ann	February 24, 1948	Mother-in-law of husband
Curry, Duncan C	May 1869	2nd great grandfather of wife of husband
Curry, Edmonia	1906	1st great grand aunt of wife of husband
Curry, Elizabeth "Bessie"	1894	1st great grand aunt of wife of husband
Curry, Emma	1854	2nd great grand aunt of wife of husband
Curry, Fortune	Abt. 1815	3rd great grandfather of wife of husband

Name:	Birth Date:	Relationship:
Curry, Frampton	1909	1st great grand uncle of wife of husband
Curry, Frank	Abt. 1935	Grand uncle of wife of husband
Curry, Frederick "Fred"	August 18, 1936	Grand uncle of wife of husband
Curry, Frederick "Freddie"	February 22, 1907	Great grandfather of wife of husband
Curry, Gabriel	1877	1st cousin 4x removed of wife of husband
Curry, Hilda	1899	1st great grand aunt of wife of husband
Curry, Ira	1895	1st great grand uncle of wife of husband
Curry, Leola	1902	1st great grand aunt of wife of husband
Curry, Lucretia "Cressie" Jo	March 05, 1929	Maternal grandmother of wife of husband
Curry, Melvalean	January 15, 1967	Wife of husband
Curry, Nancy	1930	Grand aunt of wife of husband
Curry, Pleasant	1864	1st cousin 4x removed of wife of husband
Curry, Rosa Louise	Abt. 1899	1st great grand aunt of wife of husband
Curry, Samuel	Abt. 1935	Grand uncle of wife of husband
Curry, Solomon	1904	1st great grand uncle of wife of husband
Curry, Thomas	1818	3rd great grand uncle of wife of husband
Curry, William	Abt. 1935	Grand uncle of wife of husband
Curry, William "Willie"	1892	1st great grand uncle of wife of husband
Dunbar, ?	1899	1st cousin 4x removed of wife of husband
Dunbar, William	1873	Husband of 3rd great grand aunt of wife of husband
Dunbar, William	1898	1st cousin 4x removed of wife of husband

Name:	Birth Date:	Relationship:
Dunham, ?		Husband of 2nd great grandmother of wife of husband
Durham, ?		Husband of great grandmother of wife of husband
Forsythe, Frederick	1884	1st great grand uncle of wife of husband
Forsythe, Hattie	1883	1st great grand aunt of wife of husband
Forsythe, Mildred	Abt. 1924	Grand aunt of wife of husband
Forsythe, Nelson	Abt. 1820	3rd great grandfather of wife of husband
Forsythe, Nina	Abt. 1923	Grand aunt of wife of husband
Forsythe, Percy Campbell	January 1882	Great grandfather of wife of husband
Forsythe, Robert J Washington	September 15, 1925	Maternal grandfather of wife of husband
Forsythe, Theodore	1886	1st great grand uncle of wife of husband
Forsythe, Theodore (Theopolis)	Bet. March 1855–1856	2nd great grandfather of wife of husband
Frazier, "Lillie"	1919	1st cousin 3x removed of wife of husband
Frazier, "Mamie"	1892	2nd great grand aunt of wife of husband
Frazier, "Sadie" B	1923	1st cousin 3x removed of wife of husband
Frazier, ?		5th great grandfather of wife of husband
Frazier, Andrew	1920	2nd cousin 3x removed of wife of husband
Frazier, Arthur	1909	1st cousin 3x removed of wife of husband
Frazier, Benjamin	1889	2nd great grand uncle of wife of husband
Frazier, Benjamin	1904	1st cousin 4x removed of wife of husband

Name:	Birth Date:	Relationship:
Frazier, Benjamin "Ben"	1867	3rd great grand uncle of wife of husband
Frazier, Bernice	1921	2nd cousin 3x removed of wife of husband
Frazier, Betty	1861	3rd great grand aunt of wife of husband
Frazier, Butler	1898	1st cousin 4x removed of wife of husband
Frazier, Butler	1925	2nd cousin 3x removed of wife of husband
Frazier, Clinton King	1922	1st cousin 4x removed of wife of husband
Frazier, Darthean	1929	2nd cousin 3x removed of wife of husband
Frazier, Eliza	1889	1st cousin 4x removed of wife of husband
Frazier, Eria	1916	1st cousin 3x removed of wife of husband
Frazier, Garling	1928	2nd cousin 3x removed of wife of husband
Frazier, Helen	1896	2nd great grand aunt of wife of husband
Frazier, Henry	1899	1st cousin 4x removed of wife of husband
Frazier, James E	1919	1st cousin 4x removed of wife of husband
Frazier, James N	1926	1st cousin 3x removed of wife of husband
Frazier, John W	1893	2nd great grand uncle of wife of husband
Frazier, Josephine "Josie"	1879	3rd great grand aunt of wife of husband
Frazier, Laura	1923	2nd cousin 3x removed of wife of husband

Name:	Birth Date:	Relationship:
Frazier, Lee G	1928	1st cousin 3x removed of wife of husband
Frazier, Mary	1857	3rd great grand aunt of wife of husband
Frazier, Minnie	1881	2nd great grand aunt of wife of husband
Frazier, Nancy	1865	3rd great grand aunt of wife of husband
Frazier, Nancy	1889	2nd great grandmother of wife of husband
Frazier, Robert	1884	2nd great grand uncle of wife of husband
Frazier, Rose	1891	1st cousin 4x removed of wife of husband
Frazier, Samuel	1882	2nd great grand uncle of wife of husband
Frazier, Samuel	1918	1st cousin 4x removed of wife of husband
Frazier, Samuel "Sam"	July 1854	3rd great grandfather of wife of husband
Frazier, Sidney	1863	3rd great grand uncle of wife of husband
Frazier, Smart	Abt. 1821	4th great grandfather of wife of husband
Frazier, Susan	1881	3rd great grand aunt of wife of husband
Frazier, Susan	1902	2nd great grand aunt of wife of husband
Frazier, Taylor	1859	3rd great grand uncle of wife of husband
Frazier, Tenor	1874	3rd great grand aunt of wife of husband
Frazier, Virginia	1929	2nd cousin 3x removed of wife of husband

Name:	Birth Date:	Relationship:
Frazier, William	1927	2nd cousin 3x removed of wife of husband
Frazier, William "Willie"	1898	1st cousin 4x removed of wife of husband
Frazier, William "Willie"	1898	2nd great grand uncle of wife of husband
Frazier, William "Willie" King	1917	1st cousin 4x removed of wife of husband
Gillison, "Tillie"	1900	1st cousin 3x removed of wife of husband
Gillison, ?		Husband of 2nd great grand aunt of wife of husband
Glover?, Lina	January 1872	3rd great grandmother of wife of husband
Gould, ?		Husband of 1st great grand aunt of wife of husband
Grant, ?		Husband of 1st great grand aunt of wife of husband
Green, ?		Husband of aunt of wife of husband
Hall, Susan		Wife of 1st great grand uncle of wife of husband
Hapton, Elizabeth	Abt. 1825	3rd great grandmother of wife of husband
Harris, ?		Husband of aunt of wife of husband
Harris, Carrie L	1930	1st cousin of wife of husband
Harris, Sallie	1931	1st cousin of wife of husband
Hay?, Martha	1872	Wife of 3rd great grand uncle of wife of husband
Hay?, Millie?	Abt. 1852	4th great grandmother of wife of husband
Howard, ?		Husband of grand aunt of wife of husband
Jones, ?		5th great grandfather of wife of husband

Name:	Birth Date:	Relationship:
Jones, Minda	September 1832	4th great grandmother of wife of husband
Key, Mary		Wife of 1st great grand uncle of wife of husband
Mason, "Maggie"	1895	1st cousin 1x removed of wife of husband
Mason, "Mattie" May	1913	1st cousin 1x removed of wife of husband
Mason, Addie	1876	1st cousin 2x removed of wife of husband
Mason, Aggie	March 10, 1872	Grand aunt of wife of husband
Mason, Alfred	Bet. 1825–1830	2nd great grandfather of wife of husband
Mason, Alfred	1868	1st great grand uncle of wife of husband
Mason, Alonzo	1882	Grand uncle of wife of husband
Mason, Andrew	1857	1st great grand uncle of wife of husband
Mason, Anne	1878	1st cousin 2x removed of wife of husband
Mason, Anne "Annie"	1880	1st cousin 2x removed of wife of husband
Mason, Anne Lee	1907	Aunt of wife of husband
Mason, Austin	1878	Grand uncle of wife of husband
Mason, Benjamin	1878	1st cousin 2x removed of wife of husband
Mason, Bessie	1876	1st cousin 2x removed of wife of husband
Mason, Cleveland	1870	1st great grand uncle of wife of husband
Mason, Cute	1886	1st cousin 2x removed of wife of husband
Mason, Daniel	1912	1st cousin 1x removed of wife of husband

Name:	Birth Date:	Relationship:
Mason, Dicey	1876	Sibling of paternal grandfather of wife of husband
Mason, Eddie	1875	1st cousin 2x removed of wife of husband
Mason, Edward "Ned"	1847	Great grandfather of wife of husband
Mason, Ella	1886	Grand aunt of wife of husband
Mason, Flander A		Wife of 1st great grand uncle of wife of husband
Mason, Freeman	1899	1st cousin 1x removed of wife of husband
Mason, George	1861	1st great grand uncle of wife of husband
Mason, George	1926	Uncle of wife of husband
Mason, George W	1869	Grand uncle of wife of husband
Mason, Jacob "Jake"	1859	1st great grand uncle of wife of husband
Mason, James	1872	Grand uncle of wife of husband
Mason, James	1884	1st cousin 2x removed of wife of husband
Mason, James?	Abt. 1855	1st great grand uncle of wife of husband
Mason, Jane	1875	Grand aunt of wife of husband
Mason, Janice	1885	Grand aunt of wife of husband
Mason, Jefferson D	1862	1st great grand uncle of wife of husband
Mason, Jesse	1904	Uncle of wife of husband
Mason, John	1876	1st cousin 2x removed of wife of husband
Mason, John Dooly	1906	Uncle of wife of husband
Mason, Josephine	1864	1st great grand aunt of wife of husband
Mason, Linda	1856	1st great grand aunt of wife of husband
Mason, Living	Abt. 1940	Half sister of wife of husband

Name:	Birth Date:	Relationship:
Mason, Mack	September 25, 1880	Paternal grandfather of wife of husband
Mason, Mack	1914	Uncle of wife of husband
Mason, Maria	1910	Aunt of wife of husband
Mason, Martha L	1911	1st cousin 1x removed of wife of husband
Mason, Melvin	1927	Uncle of wife of husband
Mason, Mollie	1878	1st cousin 2x removed of wife of husband
Mason, Moses?	Abt. 1800	3rd great grandfather of wife of husband
Mason, Noah	1848	1st great grand uncle of wife of husband
Mason, Noah	1895	1st cousin 2x removed of wife of husband
Mason, Oliver	1888	Grand uncle of wife of husband
Mason, Omar	1898	1st cousin 2x removed of wife of husband
Mason, Plum	1874	Grand aunt of wife of husband
Mason, Reuben	1918	1st cousin 1x removed of wife of husband
Mason, Robert B	1923	Uncle of wife of husband
Mason, Thomas	1853	1st great grand uncle of wife of husband
Mason, Thomas	1880	1st cousin 2x removed of wife of husband
Mason, Viola	1897	1st cousin 2x removed of wife of husband
Mason, Willard	1905	1st cousin 1x removed of wife of husband
Mason, Willie	1890	1st cousin 2x removed of wife of husband
Mason, Willie	1899	1st cousin 2x removed of wife of husband

Name:	Birth Date:	Relationship:
Mason, Willis	1916	1st cousin 1x removed of wife of husband
Mazo, Cellina	Abt. 1969	Half sister of wife of husband
Mazo, D "Gobby"	Abt. 1965	Half sister of wife of husband
Mazo, Living		Brother-in-law of husband
Mazo, Living		Half nephew of wife of husband
Mazo, Living		Half niece of wife of husband
Mazo, Living		Stepdaughter of father-in-law of husband
Mazo, Living	Abt. 1954	Wife of father-in-law of husband
Mazo, Living	Abt. 1956	Half brother of wife of husband
Mazo, Living	1958	Half sister of wife of husband
Mazo, Living	Abt. 1959	Half brother of wife of husband
Mazo, Living	Abt. 1961	Half brother of wife of husband
Mazo, Living	Abt. 1962	Half brother of wife of husband
Mazo, Living	Abt. 1970	Half brother of wife of husband
Mazo, M	Abt. 1963	Half brother of wife of husband
Mazo, M	Abt. 1967	Half brother of wife of husband
Mazo, Ned "Eddie"	September 07, 1912	Father-in-law of husband
Middleton, Daniel	Abt. 1855	Husband of 1st great grand aunt of wife of husband
Middleton, Dicey	1899	1st cousin 2x removed of wife of husband
Middleton, Mary	1896	1st cousin 2x removed of wife of husband
Miller, ?		Husband of 1st great grand aunt of wife of husband
Moffett, Carrie		Wife of 1st great grand uncle of wife of husband
Morgan, Sallie	March 1847	2nd great grandmother of wife of husband

Name:	Birth Date:	Relationship:
Morgan, Thomas	Abt. 1820	3rd great grandfather of wife of husband
Palmer, William?		Husband of grand aunt of wife of husband
Reeves?, King		Husband of 1st great grand aunt of wife of husband
Robinson, ?		4th great grandfather of wife of husband
Robinson, Anna	1873	2nd great grand aunt of wife of husband
Robinson, Dolly	1866	2nd great grand aunt of wife of husband
Robinson, Elizabeth	1863	2nd great grand aunt of wife of husband
Robinson, Emma	1857	2nd great grand aunt of wife of husband
Robinson, John	1876	2nd great grand uncle of wife of husband
Robinson, Joseph	1855	2nd great grand uncle of wife of husband
Robinson, Mary	May 1870	2nd great grandmother of wife of husband
Robinson, Robert	July 1825	3rd great grandfather of wife of husband
Robinson, Thomas J	1916	Half 1st great grand uncle of wife of husband
Robinson, Willis	1875	2nd great grand uncle of wife of husband
Shateen, ?		3rd great grandfather of wife of husband
Shatteen, Anne	Abt. 1865	Great grandmother of wife of husband
Shatteen, Beatrice	1915	1st cousin 2x removed of wife of husband
Shatteen, Carrie	1909	1st cousin 2x removed of wife of husband

Name:	Birth Date:	Relationship:
Shatteen, Frank	1906	1st cousin 2x removed of wife of husband
Shatteen, Isaac	1842	2nd great grand uncle of wife of husband
Shatteen, James	1866	1st great grand uncle of wife of husband
Shatteen, Jesse	1844	2nd great grand uncle of wife of husband
Shatteen, Jessie	1914	1st cousin 2x removed of wife of husband
Shatteen, Lillie	1868	1st great grand aunt of wife of husband
Shatteen, Linnie	1862	1st great grand aunt of wife of husband
Shatteen, Linnie Ann	1893	1st cousin 2x removed of wife of husband
Shatteen, Mary "Mamie"	1898	1st cousin 2x removed of wife of husband
Shatteen, Mary Jane	1900	1st cousin 2x removed of wife of husband
Shatteen, Mason	Abt. 1835	2nd great grandfather of wife of husband
Shatteen, Nathan	1912	1st cousin 2x removed of wife of husband
Shatteen, Rena	1919	1st cousin 2x removed of wife of husband
Shatteen, Virgil	1844	2nd great grand uncle of wife of husband
Shatteen, Zebedee	1916	1st cousin 2x removed of wife of husband
Stephens, Mary Ellen		Wife of 1st cousin 2x removed of wife of husband
Thompson, " Abbie"	1900	1st cousin 2x removed of wife of husband
Thompson, Adam	Abt. 1820	4th great grandfather of wife of husband

Name:	Birth Date:	Relationship:
Thompson, Catherine	1864	3rd great grand aunt of wife of husband
Thompson, Cato C	1869	1st great grand uncle of wife of husband
Thompson, Cornelius	Abt. 1874	1st great grand uncle of wife of husband
Thompson, Daniel?	1810	4th great grand uncle of wife of husband
Thompson, Ellen	1862	3rd great grand aunt of wife of husband
Thompson, Eva	May 1860	3rd great grandmother of wife of husband
Thompson, George	1854	3rd great grand uncle of wife of husband
Thompson, Henry	Abt. 1872	1st great grand uncle of wife of husband
Thompson, J J	Abt. 1872	1st great grand uncle of wife of husband
Thompson, Joshua A	1870	1st great grand uncle of wife of husband
Thompson, Julia	Abt. 1867	1st great grand aunt of wife of husband
Thompson, Larfield	1894	1st cousin 2x removed of wife of husband
Thompson, Layer	Abt. 1869	1st great grand aunt of wife of husband
Thompson, Living		Husband
Thompson, Living	February 16, 2004	Stepdaughter
Thompson, Lornie	1898	1st cousin 2x removed of wife of husband
Thompson, Maria	1856	3rd great grand aunt of wife of husband
Thompson, Peter	February 1860	Great grandfather of wife of husband
Thompson, Samuel?	Abt. 1805	3rd great grandfather of wife of husband

Name:	Birth Date:	Relationship:
Thompson, Sarah "Sallie" A Shalteen	June 1883	Paternal grandmother of wife of husband
Thompson, Seymour	1865	1st great grand uncle of wife of husband
Thompson, Stephen	Abt. 1820	2nd great grandfather of wife of husband
Thompson, Stephen	1879	1st great grand uncle of wife of husband
Thompson, Susan	1890	1st cousin 2x removed of wife of husband
Thompson, Thomas	1866	3rd great grand uncle of wife of husband
Thompson, Thomas?	1840	4th great grand uncle of wife of husband
Walker, Ellen	1850	Wife of 1st great grand uncle of wife of husband
Walker, Pheobe	1852	Wife of 1st great grand uncle of wife of husband
Washington, ?		4th great grandfather of wife of husband
Washington, ?	1910	Half 1st great grand uncle of wife of husband
Washington, Aaron	1860	2nd great grand uncle of wife of husband
Washington, Albert Ernest Robinson	1896	1st great grand uncle of wife of husband
Washington, Benjamin?	1846	3rd great grand uncle of wife of husband
Washington, Charles H Robinson	1909	1st great grand uncle of wife of husband
Washington, D C	1854	3rd great grand uncle of wife of husband
Washington, Daniel?	1842	3rd great grand uncle of wife of husband

Name:	Birth Date:	Relationship:
Washington, Dara	1898	Half 1st great grand aunt of wife of husband
Washington, Elizabeth "Betsy"	1864	2nd great grand aunt of wife of husband
Washington, Essie	1897	Half 1st great grand aunt of wife of husband
Washington, George	1902	Half 1st great grand uncle of wife of husband
Washington, Harold	April 24, 1912	Half 1st great grand uncle of wife of husband
Washington, Hasilar Neter	1876	1st cousin 4x removed of wife of husband
Washington, Joseph	1904	Half 1st great grand uncle of wife of husband
Washington, Joseph "Joe"	Abt. 1835	3rd great grandfather of wife of husband
Washington, Joseph "Joe"	Bet. September 1868–1870	2nd great grandfather of wife of husband
Washington, Lottie	1913	Half 1st great grand aunt of wife of husband
Washington, Nina	October 31, 1908	Great grandmother of wife of husband
Washington, Rose	1901	Half 1st great grand aunt of wife of husband
Washington, Samuel	1906	Half 1st great grand uncle of wife of husband
Washington, Smart	1866	2nd great grand uncle of wife of husband
Washington, Solomon	1908	Half 1st great grand uncle of wife of husband
Washington, Susan	1872	1st cousin 4x removed of wife of husband
Washington, William	1883	2nd great grand uncle of wife of husband

Name:	Birth Date:	Relationship:
Washington, William "Billie"	1905	Half 1st great grand uncle of wife of husband
Wicker, Leila		Wife of grand uncle of wife of husband
Williams, Emery Ardel		Half brother of wife of husband
Williams, Living		Half nephew of wife of husband
Williams, Living		Half nephew of wife of husband
Williams, Living		Half nephew of wife of husband
Williams, Living		Husband of mother-in-law of husband
Williams, Living		Half niece of wife of husband
Williams, Living		Half nephew of wife of husband
Williams, Living		Husband of half sister of wife of husband
Williams, Living		Half nephew of wife of husband
Williams, Living		Half nephew of wife of husband
Williams, Living		Half nephew of wife of husband
Williams, Living		Half sister of wife of husband
Williams, Living		Half sister of wife of husband
Williams, Living		Half sister of wife of husband
Williams, Living		Half brother of wife of husband

Chapter Five

Our family's calendar.

Important annual dates of birth, marriage and death and possible data errors to be corrected.

January 2013

January 2013

S	M	T	W	T	F	S
		1	2	3	4	5
6	7	8	9	10	11	12
13	14	15	16	17	18	19
20	21	22	23	24	25	26
27	28	29	30	31		

Sun	Mon	Tue	Wed	Thu	Fri	Sat
		1	2	3	4	5
6	7	8	9	10	11	12
13	14	15 Melvalean Curry	16	17	18	19 Percy C. Forsythe
20	21	22	23	24	25 Eva Thompson	26
27	28	29	30	31		

February 2013

Sun	Mon	Tue	Wed	Thu	Fri	Sat
					1	2
3	4	5	6	7	8 Charles ". Curry	9
10	11	12	13	14	15	16 Living Thompson
17	18	19	20	21	22 Frederick ". Curry	23
24 Delores A. Curry	25	26	27	28		

March 2013

March 2013

S	M	T	W	T	F	S
					1	2
3	4	5	6	7	8	9
10	11	12	13	14	15	16
17	18	19	20	21	22	23
24	25	26	27	28	29	30
31						

Sun	Mon	Tue	Wed	Thu	Fri	Sat
					1	2
3	4	5 Lucretia ".J. Curry	6	7	8	9
10 Aggie Mason	11	12	13	14	15	16
17	18	19 Samuel ". Frazier	20	21 Sarah ".A.S. Thompson	22	23
24	25	26	27	28	29	30
31						

April 2013

April 2013

S	M	T	W	T	F	S
	1	2	3	4	5	6
7	8	9	10	11	12	13
14	15	16	17	18	19	20
21	22	23	24	25	26	27
28	29	30				

Sun	Mon	Tue	Wed	Thu	Fri	Sat
	1	2	3	4	5	6
7 Eva M. Brown	8	9	10	11	12	13
14	15	16	17 Lucretia Curry and Robert	18	19	20
21	22	23	24 Harold Washington	25	26	27
28	29 Mary	30				

May 2013

May 2013

S	M	T	W	T	F	S
			1	2	3	4
5	6	7	8	9	10	11
12	13	14	15	16	17	18
19	20	21	22	23	24	25
26	27	28	29	30	31	

Sun	Mon	Tue	Wed	Thu	Fri	Sat
			1	2 Pheobe Walker and	3	4
5	6	7	8	9	10	11
12	13	14 Eva M. Brown	15	16	17	18
19 Anne Shatteen and	20	21	22	23 Theodore (. Forsythe	24	25
26	27 Charlotte Andrews and	28	29 Melvalean Curry	30	31	

June 2013

June 2013

S	M	T	W	T	F	S
						1
2	3	4	5	6	7	8
9	10	11	12	13	14	15
16	17	18	19	20	21	22
23	24	25	26	27	28	29
30						

Sun	Mon	Tue	Wed	Thu	Fri	Sat
						1
2	3 Duncan C. Curry	4 Frederick ". Curry	5	6 Elizabeth Brown	7	8
9	10	11	12	13	14	15
16	17	18	19	20	21	22 Ellen Walker and Andrew
23	24	25	26	27	28	29
30						

July 2013

July 2013

S	M	T	W	T	F	S
	1	2	3	4	5	6
7	8	9	10	11	12	13
14	15	16	17	18	19	20
21	22	23	24	25	26	27
28	29	30	31			

Sun	Mon	Tue	Wed	Thu	Fri	Sat
	1	2	3	4	5 Joseph ". Brown	6
7	8	9	10	11	12	13
14	15	16	17	18	19	20
21	22	23	24	25	26	27
28	29	30	31			

August 2013

August 2013

S	M	T	W	T	F	S
				1	2	3
4	5	6	7	8	9	10
11	12	13	14	15	16	17
18	19	20	21	22	23	24
25	26	27	28	29	30	31

Sun	Mon	Tue	Wed	Thu	Fri	Sat
				1	2	3
4	5 Nina Washington	6	7	8	9	10
11	12	13	14	15 Benjamin ". Alston	16	17
18 Frederick ". Curry	19	20	21	22	23	24
25	26	27	28	29	30	31

September 2013

Sun	Mon	Tue	Wed	Thu	Fri	Sat
1	2	3	4	5	6	7 Ned ". Mazo
8	9	10	11	12	13	14
15 Robert J.W. Forsythe	16	17 Elizabeth Brown and	18 Mack Mason	19	20	21
22	23	24	25 Mack Mason	26	27	28
29	30					

October 2013

October 2013

S	M	T	W	T	F	S
		1	2	3	4	5
6	7	8	9	10	11	12
13	14	15	16	17	18	19
20	21	22	23	24	25	26
27	28	29	30	31		

Sun	Mon	Tue	Wed	Thu	Fri	Sat
		1	2	3	4	5
6	7	8	9	10	11	12
13	14	15	16 Elizabeth Brown	17	18	19
20	21	22	23	24	25	26
27 Ella L. Brown	28	29	30	31 Nina Washington		

November 2013

Sun	Mon	Tue	Wed	Thu	Fri	Sat
					1	2
3	4	5	6	7	8	9
10 Sallie Morgan	11	12	13 Frederick ". Curry	14 Harold Washington	15	16
17	18 Ellen Adams and Jacob ".	19	20	21 Melvalean Curry and	22 Robert J.W. Forsythe	23
24	25 Harriet Cumming and	26	27	28	29	30 Joseph ". Washington

December 2013

Sun	Mon	Tue	Wed	Thu	Fri	Sat
1	2	3	4	5 Nina Forsythe	6	7
8 Ella L. Brown	9 Leila Wicker and Austin	10 Lucretia ".J. Curry	11	12	13 Joseph ". Brown	14
15 Sarah Thompson	16 Martha Clayton and Delores A. Curry	17	18	19	20 Ned ". Mazo	21
22	23	24 Lavinia ? and George W.	25	26	27 Susan Hall and James	28 Bessie Mason and Henry
29	30	31				

Possible Data Errors

Name	Birth Date	Potential Error
?		The birth date is missing. The marriage date is missing.
?		The birth date is missing. The marriage date is missing.
?		The birth date is missing. The marriage date is missing.
?		The birth date is missing. The marriage date is missing.
?		The birth date is missing. The marriage date is missing.
?		The birth date is missing. The marriage date is missing.
?		The birth date is missing. The marriage date is missing.
?		The birth date is missing. The marriage date is missing.
?		The birth date is missing. The marriage date is missing.
?		The birth date is missing. The marriage date is missing.
?		The birth date is missing. The marriage date is missing.
?		The birth date is missing. The marriage date is missing.
?		The birth date is missing. The marriage date is missing.
?		The birth date is missing. The marriage date is missing.
?		The birth date is missing. The marriage date is missing.
?		The birth date is missing. The marriage date is missing.
?		The birth date is missing. The marriage date is missing.
?		The birth date is missing. The marriage date is missing.
?		The birth date is missing. The marriage date is missing.
?		The birth date is missing. The marriage date is missing.
?		The birth date is missing. The marriage date is missing.
?		The birth date is missing.
?		The birth date is missing. The marriage date is missing.
?		The birth date is missing. The marriage date is missing.

Name	Birth Date	Potential Error
?		The birth date is missing. The marriage date is missing.
?		The birth date is missing. The marriage date is missing.
?		The birth date is missing. The marriage date is missing.
?		The birth date is missing. The marriage date is missing.
Anna ?	1883	The marriage date is missing.
Anne ?	1907	The marriage date is missing.
?		The birth date is missing.
Grace ?		The birth date is missing. The marriage date is missing.
Hilda ?	1870	The marriage date is missing.
Judy ?	1856	The marriage date is missing.
Julia ?		The birth date is missing. The marriage date is missing.
Julia ?	1910	The marriage date is missing.
?		The birth date is missing. The marriage date is missing.
Lucy ?		The birth date is missing. The marriage date is missing.
Lula "Lou" ?	1872	The name may include a nickname. The marriage date is missing.
Mabel ?	1903	The marriage date is missing.
Minda ?	1855	The marriage date is missing.
Minnie ?	1897	The marriage date is missing.
Nellie ?	1894	The marriage date is missing.
Nora ?	1889	The marriage date is missing.
Rhinor? ?	Abt. 1800	The marriage date is missing.
Stella ?	1885	The marriage date is missing.
?		The birth date is missing. The marriage date is missing.
?		The birth date is missing. The marriage date is missing.
? Alston		The birth date is missing. The marriage date is missing.
Albert Alston	1874	The marriage date is missing.
Benjamin "Ben" Alston	August 1845	The name may include a nickname.
Elizabeth "Bessie" Alston	December 1870	The name may include a nickname.
Charlotte Andrews		The birth date is missing.
Dorothy Mae Brown	Abt. 1920	The marriage date is missing.
Ella Lee Brown	October 27, 1921	The marriage date is missing.
Eva Mae Brown	May 14, 1924	The marriage date is missing.
James Brown	1880	The marriage date is missing.
Joseph "Joe" Brown	September 1871	The name may include a nickname.
Joseph "Joe" Brown	July 05, 1890	The name may include a nickname.
Lillian "Lillie" Brown	Abt. 1920	The name may include a nickname.
Samuel? Brown	Abt. 1800	The marriage date is missing.

Name	Birth Date	Potential Error
Mary Chapman		The birth date is missing. The marriage date is missing.
Harriet Cumming		The birth date is missing.
Henry Cumming		The birth date is missing.
Charles "Charlie" Curry	February 08, 1912	The name may include a nickname.
Elizabeth "Bessie" Curry	1894	The name may include a nickname.
Frederick "Fred" Curry	August 18, 1936	The name may include a nickname.
Frederick "Freddie" Curry	February 22, 1907	The name may include a nickname.
Lucretia "Cressie" Jo Curry	March 05, 1929	The name may include a nickname.
Solomon Curry	1904	The marriage date is missing.
Thomas Curry	1818	The marriage date is missing.
William "Willie" Curry	1892	The name may include a nickname. The marriage date is missing.
William Dunbar	1873	The marriage date is missing.
? Dunham		The birth date is missing. The marriage date is missing.
? Durham		The birth date is missing.
Mildred Forsythe	Abt. 1924	The marriage date is missing.
Theodore Forsythe	1886	The marriage date is missing.
Theodore (Theopolis) Forsythe	Bet. March 1855–1856	The name may include a nickname.
"Lillie" Frazier	1919	The name may include a nickname.
"Mamie" Frazier	1892	The name may include a nickname.
"Sadie" B Frazier	1923	The name may include a nickname.
? Frazier		The birth date is missing. The marriage date is missing.
Benjamin Frazier	1889	The marriage date is missing.
Benjamin "Ben" Frazier	1867	The name may include a nickname. The marriage date is missing.
Butler Frazier	1898	The marriage date is missing.
Henry Frazier	1899	The marriage date is missing.
Josephine "Josie" Frazier	1879	The name may include a nickname. The marriage date is missing.
Minnie Frazier	1881	The marriage date is missing.
Robert Frazier	1884	The marriage date is missing.
Samuel "Sam" Frazier	July 1854	The name may include a nickname.
Taylor Frazier	1859	The marriage date is missing.
William "Willie" Frazier	1898	The name may include a nickname. The marriage date is missing.
William "Willie" Frazier	1898	The name may include a nickname.
William "Willie" King Frazier	1917	The name may include a nickname.
"Tillie" Gillison	1900	The name may include a nickname.
? Gillison		The birth date is missing. The marriage date is missing.
? Gould		The birth date is missing. The marriage date is missing.
? Grant		The birth date is missing. The marriage date is missing.
? Green		The birth date is missing. The marriage date is missing.

Name	Birth Date	Potential Error
Susan Hall		The birth date is missing.
? Harris		The birth date is missing.
		The marriage date is missing.
Martha Hay?	1872	The marriage date is missing.
? Howard		The birth date is missing.
		The marriage date is missing.
? Jones		The birth date is missing.
		The marriage date is missing.
Mary Key		The birth date is missing.
"Maggie" Mason	1895	The name may include a nickname.
		The marriage date is missing.
"Mattie" May Mason	1913	The name may include a nickname.
Aggie Mason	March 10, 1872	The marriage date is missing.
Anne "Annie" Mason	1880	The name may include a nickname.
Anne Lee Mason	1907	The marriage date is missing.
Edward "Ned" Mason	1847	The name may include a nickname.
Flander A Mason		The birth date is missing.
George W Mason	1869	The marriage date is missing.
Jacob "Jake" Mason	1859	The name may include a nickname.
Josephine Mason	1864	The marriage date is missing.
Moses? Mason	Abt. 1800	The marriage date is missing.
Living Mazo		The birth date is missing.
D "Gobby" Mazo	Abt. 1965	The name may include a nickname.
Living Mazo		The birth date is missing.
Ned "Eddie" Mazo	September 07, 1912	The name may include a nickname.
Living Mazo		The birth date is missing.
Living Mazo	1958	The marriage date is missing.
Living Mazo		The birth date is missing.
Living Mazo	Abt. 1954	The marriage date is missing.
? Miller		The birth date is missing.
		The marriage date is missing.
Carrie Moffett		The birth date is missing.
William? Palmer		The birth date is missing.
		The marriage date is missing.
King Reeves?		The birth date is missing.
		The marriage date is missing.
? Robinson		The birth date is missing.
		The marriage date is missing.
? Shateen		The birth date is missing.
		The marriage date is missing.
James Shatteen	1866	The marriage date is missing.
Mary "Mamie" Shatteen	1898	The name may include a nickname.
Mary Ellen Stephens		The birth date is missing.
" Abbie" Thompson	1900	The name may include a nickname.
Joshua A Thompson	1870	The marriage date is missing.
Living Thompson		The birth date is missing.
Samuel? Thompson	Abt. 1805	The marriage date is missing.
Sarah "Sallie" A Shalteen Thompson	June 1883	The name may include a nickname.

Name	Birth Date	Potential Error
? Washington		The birth date is missing. The marriage date is missing.
D C Washington	1854	The marriage date is missing.
Elizabeth "Betsy" Washington	1864	The name may include a nickname.
Joseph "Joe" Washington	Bet. September 1868–1870	The name may include a nickname.
Joseph "Joe" Washington	Abt. 1835	The name may include a nickname.
William "Billie" Washington	1905	The name may include a nickname.
Leila Wicker		The birth date is missing.
Living Williams		The birth date is missing. The marriage date is missing.
Living Williams		The birth date is missing.
Living Williams		The birth date is missing.
Living Williams		The birth date is missing. The marriage date is missing.
Emery Ardel Williams		The birth date is missing.
Living Williams		The birth date is missing.
Living Williams		The birth date is missing.
Living Williams		The individual has the same last name as her husband, Living Williams. The birth date is missing. The marriage date is missing.
Living Williams		The birth date is missing. The marriage date is missing.
Living Williams		The birth date is missing. The marriage date is missing.
Living Williams		The birth date is missing. The marriage date is missing.
Living Williams		The birth date is missing.
Living Williams		The birth date is missing.
Living Williams		The birth date is missing.
Living Williams		The birth date is missing.

Afterword

Without my ancestors, I would have been had the chance to experience the wonders of life. Thank you grandma and grandpa, you have allowed me to see beautiful places, do wonderful things and meet amazing people. This is my testament.

Source Bibliography

"Annie" Gilmartin. Source Medium: Book

? household. Source Medium: Book

12,000 Ancestors.

500 Years of Wittels and Related Families. Source Medium: Book

A Potrait of Our Ancestors. Source Medium: Book

A. Maria Herrold. Source Medium: Book

A.K. Burgert. Source Medium: Book

Abel F Thompson.

Abel R Thompson. Source Medium: Book

Abel Robert Thompson.

Abel Thompson death certificate. Source Medium: Book

Abel Thompson. Source Medium: Book

Abraham Gaugler death certificate. Source Medium: Book

Abraham Gaugler.

Abraham Joray. Source Medium: Book

Abraham Jury. Source Medium: Book

Abraham Shora. Source Medium: Book

Abraham Shorah.

Abraham Zora. Source Medium: Book

Abram Joray. Source Medium: Book

Acra household. Source Medium: Book

Acri family information.

Acri household. Source Medium: Book

Acri-Curcio marriage record. Source Medium: Book

Adam Faber.

Adam Frantz. Source Medium: Book

Adam Gice. Source Medium: Book

Adam Gise.

Adam Guise. Source Medium: Book

Adam Piper.

Adam Wirth.

Adeline Row. Source Medium: Book

Aemilius Acri.

Aggie Palmer.

Agnes Harvey Piper.

Albert E Wittle death certificate. Source Medium: Book

Albert E Wittle Sr. Source Medium: Book

Albert E Wittle. Source Medium: Book

Albert E. Wittle. Source Medium: Book

Albert Wittle.

Alexander Thompson. Source Medium: Book

Allston household.

Alston household.

Amel Acri. Source Medium: Book

Amel F Acri death certificate. Source Medium: Book

Amel F Acri. Source Medium: Book

Amel F. Acri. Source Medium: Book

Ancestors of John Wedgewood White.

Ancestors of Richard Alan Lebo. Source Medium: Book

Ancestry Public Tree.

Anderson family information. Source Medium: Book

Anderson household. Source Medium: Book

Anderson-Keefer marriage record. Source Medium: Book

And'r Emrich.

Andreas Emrich.

Andreas Hansel. Source Medium: Book

Andreas Messerschmidt. Source Medium: Book

Andreas Messersmith.

Andreas Miller. Source Medium: Book

Andrew Emerick. Source Medium: Book

Andrew Gise Hensel death certificate. Source Medium: Book

Andrew Gise Hensel. Source Medium: Book

Andrew Hensel. Source Medium: Book

Andrew Hentzell. Source Medium: Book

Andrew Henzel.

Andrew Messerschmidt.

Andrew Miller. Source Medium: Book

Angela Romano.

Angelo Camone.

Angelo Carmona.

Angelo Carmone.

Angst Family Information.

Angst household. Source Medium: Book

Anna Carmona. Source Medium: Book

Anna Catherina Heck. Source Medium: Book

Anna Catherine Heck. Source Medium: Book

Anna Charlotte Or.

Anna Eliza Shover. Source Medium: Book

Anna Eliza. Shover. Source Medium: Book

Anna Guniunda Gubern.

Anna Kinugonda Stupp.

Anna M Herrold Arnold. Source Medium: Book

Anna Margaret Gabel. Source Medium: Book

Anna Margaretha Gruber.

Anna Margaretha Miller. Source Medium: Book

Anna Margaretha Zimmerman.

Anna Maria Arnold. Source Medium: Book

Anna Maria Eva Long. Source Medium: Book

Anna Maria Hamm. Source Medium: Book

Anna Maria Heilze. Source Medium: Book

Anna Mary Elizabeth Benesch. Source Medium: Book

Anna Romano.

Anna Shover.

Anna Wittel. Source Medium: Book

Anne Naughton.

April's Ancestors. Source Medium: Book

Arnold family information. Source Medium: Book

Arnold family. Source Medium: Book

Arnold household. Source Medium: Book

Baddorf family information. Source Medium: Book

Baddorf Family. Source Medium: Book

Baddorf household. Source Medium: Book

Badorf household. Source Medium: Book

Badorf Jr household. Source Medium: Book

Badorf Sr household. Source Medium: Book

Balser Ramberger.

Balthaser Bordner. Source Medium: Book

Balthaser Bortner. Source Medium: Book

Balthaser Pauley Bortner. Source Medium: Book

Balthaser Romberger.

Baltzer Romberger. Source Medium: Book

Bank household.

Barbara Rowe. Source Medium: Book

Barbush household. Source Medium: Book

Barbusha household.

Bardner household. Source Medium: Book

Barr Genealogy & Related Families.

Barrett household. Source Medium: Book

Bartel Raumberger. Source Medium: Book

Bastoe household. Source Medium: Book

Batdorf data.

Batdorf Family information. Source Medium: Book

Batdorf household. Source Medium: Book

Batdorf household. Source Medium: Book

Batdorf household. Source Medium: Book

Batdorf-Wert marriage record. Source Medium: Book

Batlthasar Bordner. Source Medium: Book

Batrdorf household. Source Medium: Book

Baugher family information. Source Medium: Book

Baugher household. Source Medium: Book

Beal household.

Beall household.

Beall-Hinson marriage.

Ben Alston.

Benfield Family information. Source Medium: Book

Benjamin Alston.

Berks County Early Church Records.

Berks County marriage records. Source Medium: Book

Beulah Batdorf. Source Medium: Book

Beulah I Batdorf death certificate. Source Medium: Book

Beulah I Batdorf. Source Medium: Book

Bible p. Source Medium: Book

Bob Averell Family Tree. Source Medium: Book

Bodorff household. Source Medium: Book

Bolich household. Source Medium: Book

Bordner family information. Source Medium: Book

Bordner household (Henry). Source Medium: Book

Bordner household. Source Medium: Book

Bordorf household. Source Medium: Book

Bortner family information. Source Medium: Book

Bortner-Velt marriage record. Source Medium: Book

Bottorff household. Source Medium: Book

Bowerman family. Source Medium: Book

Brown family information. Source Medium: Book

Brown household. Source Medium: Book

Brubaker household. Source Medium: Book

Bucher household. Source Medium: Book

Bucher information. Source Medium: Book

Bucker household. Source Medium: Book

Buela/Buglio Family.

Burials 1782-1807.

Camillo Carmone.

Capser Hensel. Source Medium: Book

Carmina "Catarina" Buglio. Source Medium: Book

Carmine Mario "Francesco" Buglio. Source Medium: Book

Carmona-Romano family information.

Caspar Haenssel. Source Medium: Book

Caspar Hentsell. Source Medium: Book

Casper Arnold Senior. Source Medium: Book

Casper Arnold Sr. Source Medium: Book

Casper Arnold, Senior. Source Medium: Book

Casper Arnold. Source Medium: Book

Casper Hansel. Source Medium: Book

Casper Hensel. Source Medium: Book

Casper Hentzel. Source Medium: Book

Cath. Anderson. Source Medium: Book

Catharina Arnold. Source Medium: Book

Catharine Anderson.

Catharine Swartz. Source Medium: Book

Cather Gissemenen.

Catherine (Mary Kate) Wittle. Source Medium: Book

Catherine Anderson. Source Medium: Book

Catherine Duncan. Source Medium: Book

Catherine Wert.

Catherine Whittle death certificate. Source Medium: Book

Catherine Wittle. Source Medium: Book

Central PA Families. Source Medium: Book

Cewlin household. Source Medium: Book

Ceynis Shannon. Source Medium: Book

Charles A Fsiher, p 40, p 81, Snyder County Pioneers.

Charley Duncan.

Charlotte Layman.

Chesebro' genealogy. Source Medium: Book

Children of Johann Michael Emerich. Source Medium: Book

Christian Gruber. Source Medium: Book

Churches Between the Mountains.

Clara Hensel. Source Medium: Book

Clara M Hensel death certificate. Source Medium: Book

Clay/Klees, Nesbit, etc. Source Medium: Book

Colored boy.

Connor family information. Source Medium: Book

Connor household. Source Medium: Book

Conrad Mantz.

Conrad Updegrove.

Cressie Curry death certificate. Source Medium: Book

Cressie Curry. Source Medium: Book

Cressie Mazo.

Croce/Walker Family Tree. Source Medium: Book

Crossley, Gunsallus, Kimmel Family Trees. Source Medium: Book

Culin family information. Source Medium: Book

Culin household. Source Medium: Book

Culin-Taylor marriage. Source Medium: Book

Culnan household. Source Medium: Book

Culp household. Source Medium: Book

Cuniganda Gruber. Source Medium: Book

Curry household. Source Medium: Book

Curry-Brown marriage.

Cyrus J Shannon.

Cyrus Shannon death certificate. Source Medium: Book

Cyrus Shannon. Source Medium: Book

Cyrus W Shannon. Source Medium: Book

Daniel Angst.

Daniel Keefer. Source Medium: Book

Daniel R Piper.

Daniel Row. Source Medium: Book

Daniel Rowe. Source Medium: Book

Daniel Updegrave. Source Medium: Book

Daniel Updegrove death certificate. Source Medium: Book

Daniel Updegrove. Source Medium: Book

Dauphin County Names.

David Kieffer. Source Medium: Book

David McCloud.

David Penman. Source Medium: Book

David R. Layman. Source Medium: Book

David Stoddard. Source Medium: Book

David Stoddart. Source Medium: Book

David Wert (West) death record. Source Medium: Book

David Wert death certificate. Source Medium: Book

David Wert. Source Medium: Book

Death of Balthaser Bordner. Source Medium: Book

Decsendants of Jakob Herrold.

Deibler family information. Source Medium: Book

Delored Curry death cerrtificate.

Delored Curry death certificate.

Descedants of Emmerich. Source Medium: Book

Descedants of Herman OpDenGraeff. Source Medium: Book

Descedants of Jakob Herrold.

Descedants of Martin Stupp.

Descendants of Balthaser Pauley Bortner. Source Medium: Book

Descendants of Christian Gruber.

Descendants of Frederick Adam Faber.

Descendants of Henry Gruber.

Descendants of Herman Op den Graef. Source Medium: Book

Descendants of Jakob Herrold.

Descendants of Johann Georg Gauckler. Source Medium: Book

Descendants of Johann Pfannebecker. Source Medium: Book

Descendants of Michael Garman. Source Medium: Book

Descendants of Philip Jacob Bortner. Source Medium: Book

Descendants of Valentine Ney. Source Medium: Book

Deterick Wertz.

Dieter Wurtz.

Dininni Book. Source Medium: Book

Direct Descendants of John Bartholomus Romberger to Roger Cramer. Source Medium: Book

Direct Descendants of John Bartholomus Romberger. Source Medium: Book

Don Moyer.

Donkert household. Source Medium: Book

Dorothy Gaugler. Source Medium: Book

Dunbar household.

Duncan Curry.

Duncan family information. Source Medium: Book

Duncan household. Source Medium: Book

Duncan-Layman mariage record. Source Medium: Book

Duncan-Layman marriage record. Source Medium: Book

Dungan household. Source Medium: Book

Dungard household. Source Medium: Book

Dunham household.

Eddie Mazo. Source Medium: Book

Edward Mason death certificate. Source Medium: Book

Edward Mason. Source Medium: Book

Elijah Anderson. Source Medium: Book

Elizabeth Batdorf. Source Medium: Book

Elizabeth Curry.

Elizabeth Kelly. Source Medium: Book

Elizabeth Minnich.

Elizabeth Penman.

Elizabeth Scheetz.

Elizabeth Updegroff.

Elizabeth Wert death record. Source Medium: Book

Elmira Layman. Source Medium: Book

Ely household. Source Medium: Book

Emerich household.

Emerick family information. Source Medium: Book

Emma Andersen. Source Medium: Book

Emma L. Anderson. Source Medium: Book

Emma L. Keefer. Source Medium: Book

Emma Louisa Anderson death certificate. Source Medium: Book

Emma Louisa Anderson. Source Medium: Book

Emma Louisa Keefer.

Emrich household. Source Medium: Book

Emrick household. Source Medium: Book

Epley household. Source Medium: Book

Eppley household. Source Medium: Book

Erasmo Vitale.

European Origin of the Herrolds (Herolds). Source Medium: Book

Eva Arnold Keefer. Source Medium: Book

Eva Elisabeth Schnug. Source Medium: Book

Eva Elizabeth Schnug Wirth. Source Medium: Book

Eva Frazier.

Faber household. Source Medium: Book

Faber. Source Medium: Book

Family of Eldon G. Keefer. Source Medium: Book

Family Ties. Source Medium: Book

Faver household. Source Medium: Book

Fawper household. Source Medium: Book

Fawver household. Source Medium: Book

Felice Vitale.

Felty family information. Source Medium: Book

Felty Family record. Source Medium: Book

Felty household. Source Medium: Book

Felty Welker. Source Medium: Book

Fidler. Source Medium: Book

Forsyth household.

Forsyth-Curry marriage.

Forsythe household.

Fraisier household.

Francesco Acri. Source Medium: Book

Francis Rou.

Francis Row. Source Medium: Book

Francis Rowe.

Franjensco Acri. Source Medium: Book

Frank (Rau) Rowe. Source Medium: Book

Frank Acri death certificate. Source Medium: Book

Frank Acri.

Frank Rowe. Source Medium: Book

Frantz household. Source Medium: Book

Frantz. Source Medium: Book

Franz household. Source Medium: Book

Franz-Gieseman marriage record. Source Medium: Book

Fraser household.

Frazier household.

Fred Duncan.

Freddie Curry.

Frey household. Source Medium: Book

Frontz household. Source Medium: Book

Fry household. Source Medium: Book

Furey Bretz Family Tree. Source Medium: Book

Gable household. Source Medium: Book

Gaetano Barbuscio. Source Medium: Book

Garman household. Source Medium: Book

Garmon household. Source Medium: Book

Gaucker household. Source Medium: Book

Gaugler family information. Source Medium: Book

Gaugler household. Source Medium: Book

Gaugler Notes. Source Medium: Book

Geeseman household. Source Medium: Book

Geip family information. Source Medium: Book

Geipe household. Source Medium: Book

Geipp-Schreiberin marriage record. Source Medium: Book

Genealogy data p 128 (Family pp). Source Medium: Book

Geo Felty.

Geo Gaugler. Source Medium: Book

Geo. Gaugler, Jr. Source Medium: Book

George Arnold. Source Medium: Book

George Arnolt.

George Culin. Source Medium: Book

George Gaugler. Source Medium: Book

George H Layman. Source Medium: Book

George H Leyman. Source Medium: Book

George Herold.

George Herrold. Source Medium: Book

George Hoke.

George John Felty. Source Medium: Book

George Justys Culin. Source Medium: Book

George Peiffer.

George Piper.

George Schuetz.

George Schup. Source Medium: Book

George Schupp. Source Medium: Book

George Sheets death record. Source Medium: Book

George Sheets Jr. Source Medium: Book

George Sheets. Source Medium: Book

George Sheetz.

George Shitz. Source Medium: Book

George Shutz. Source Medium: Book

George W Brown.

George William Baugher. Source Medium: Book

Gerald Gilbert Thompson birth record. Source Medium: Book

Gerald Gilbert Thompson.

German household. Source Medium: Book

Gese household. Source Medium: Book

Geseman household. Source Medium: Book

Gibe household. Source Medium: Book

Gieseman family information. Source Medium: Book

Gieseman household. Source Medium: Book

Gilmartin Household.

Gilmartin-Naughten.

Gipe family information. Source Medium: Book

Gipe Family of Chanceford Twp., York Co. Source Medium: Book

Gipe household. Source Medium: Book

Gipe/Geib/Geiep,York Co, PA. Source Medium: Book

Gise household. Source Medium: Book

Giuseppa Quintavalle.

Giuseppe Romano.

Giuseppina Magnelli. Source Medium: Book

Goodman household. Source Medium: Book

Goose household. Source Medium: Book

Gottleib Zinck. Source Medium: Book

Gottleib Zink. Source Medium: Book

Gougler household. Source Medium: Book

Gougler/Thursby family information.

Gouter Household.

Gruber family information. Source Medium: Book

Gruber-Stulp marriage record. Source Medium: Book

GUESMAN-L.

Guise household. Source Medium: Book

Gusman household. Source Medium: Book

Gussie M. Thompson. Source Medium: Book

Gussie Mae Thompson.

Gussie May Hensel. Source Medium: Book

Gussie May Thompson death certificate. Source Medium: Book

Gussie May Thompson. Source Medium: Book

Gussie Thompson. Source Medium: Book

Guyer household. Source Medium: Book

Haldeman household. Source Medium: Book

Hannah Artilla Duncan.

Harman household. Source Medium: Book

Harper B Thompson death certificate. Source Medium: Book

Harper B Thompson. Source Medium: Book

Harper Bruce Thompson birth record. Source Medium: Book

Harper household.

Harper Thompson. Source Medium: Book

Harry Duncan.

Hawkins household. Source Medium: Book

Heheel household. Source Medium: Book

Heintzelman Family Information.

Henrich Wolffskehl. Source Medium: Book

Henry Boucher.

Henry Bucher. Source Medium: Book

Henry Curry.

Henry Fry.

Henry Klein. Source Medium: Book

Henry Minich.

Henry Minick.

Henry Minnick death record. Source Medium: Book

Henry Minnick.

Henry Neal. Source Medium: Book

Henry Neel. Source Medium: Book

Henry W Bucher Sr. Source Medium: Book

Henry Wertz.

Henry Wolffskeil.

Henry Wolfsiel.

Henry Wollfkull. Source Medium: Book

Henry Woolfkull. Source Medium: Book

Hensel family information. Source Medium: Book

Hensel household. Source Medium: Book

Hensel-Workman marriage record. Source Medium: Book

Hensil household. Source Medium: Book

Hensley household. Source Medium: Book

Hentzel household. Source Medium: Book

Hentzelle household. Source Medium: Book

Henzell household. Source Medium: Book

Hergershimer household.

Herold household. Source Medium: Book

Herrold family information. Source Medium: Book

Herrold Lineage. Source Medium: Book

Hinsle household. Source Medium: Book

Hoke family data. Source Medium: Book

Hooker household.

Hoover/McHenry family. Source Medium: Book

Howard A.C. Hensel. Source Medium: Book

Howard Andrew Carson Hensel.

Hullsizer household. Source Medium: Book

Hummer family information.

Hurt household.

Hutchinson & Allied Families from East TN. Source Medium: Book

Ireneo Romano.

Irvin Duncan. Source Medium: Book

Irvin Francis Duncan death certificate. Source Medium: Book

Irvin Francis Duncan.

Irvin W Duncan.

Irvin Wilfred Francis Duncan.

Isabel Penman.

J Henry Minick.

J.M. Source Medium: Book

Jacob Bordner.

Jacob Bortner.

Jacob Emrich.

Jacob F Stewart.

Jacob Gipe. Source Medium: Book

Jacob Gype. Source Medium: Book

Jacob H Wittle.

Jacob Layman.

Jacob Leman. Source Medium: Book

Jacob Leyman. Source Medium: Book

Jacob Livezey. Source Medium: Book

Jacob Livezly.

Jacob Loyman.

Jacob Oberlander. Source Medium: Book

Jacob Rudy wife. Source Medium: Book

Jacob Rudy. Source Medium: Book

Jacob Stewart. Source Medium: Book

Jacob Wert. Source Medium: Book

Jacob Wirt.

Jacob Wirth. Source Medium: Book

Jacob Wittel. Source Medium: Book

Jacob Wittle. Source Medium: Book

Jacobi family information.

James E Batdorf. Source Medium: Book

James Edward Batdorf death certificate. Source Medium: Book

James Edward Batdorf. Source Medium: Book

James H Anderson. Source Medium: Book

James McKim.

James McKinsey. Source Medium: Book

James P Keefer death record abstract. Source Medium: Book

James P. Keefer. Source Medium: Book

Jane McKinstry. Source Medium: Book

Joahnn Jacob Leiman. Source Medium: Book

Joe Brown.

Joe Washington Jr.

Joh Martin Epple. Source Medium: Book

Johan Adam Wirth. Source Medium: Book

Johan Georg Werner.

Johan George Arnold. Source Medium: Book

Johan George Wilhelm Gussemann. Source Medium: Book

Johan Nicholas Geipp. Source Medium: Book

Johann Adam Wirth. Source Medium: Book

Johann Christian Warner. Source Medium: Book

Johann Christian Werner. Source Medium: Book

Johann Dietrich Wertz.

Johann Dietrich Wuerz. Source Medium: Book

Johann Jacob Etler.

Johann Jacob Leiman. Source Medium: Book

Johann Jacob Wittel. Source Medium: Book

Johann Schwartz data. Source Medium: Book

Johann Uptegrav. Source Medium: Book

Johann Wendel Traut.

Johann Wilhelm Frantz. Source Medium: Book

Johannes (John) Faber.

Johannes Schup. Source Medium: Book

John Adam Geiss. Source Medium: Book

John Anderson.

John B Shover death certificate.

John Bager. Source Medium: Book

John Carson Crow & Faye Garnett Woodward. Source Medium: Book

John Christopher Wider.

John Connor. Source Medium: Book

John Conrad Bucher. Source Medium: Book

John Conrad Hoke.

John E Shover. Source Medium: Book

John E Wittle. Source Medium: Book

John Faber. Source Medium: Book

John Geo. Schuetz.

John George Arnold.

John George Bager (father). Source Medium: Book

John George Felty.

John George Herrold Sr. Source Medium: Book

John George Herrold Sr. Source Medium: Book

John George Herrold. Source Medium: Book

John Henry Minick.

John Henry Wert.

John Jacob Emerich.

John Jacob Wirth.

John Lindermuth. Source Medium: Book

John Martin Louis Stewart. Source Medium: Book

John Mertz (Wertz).

John Miller.

John Penman. Source Medium: Book

John Peters. Source Medium: Book

John Reiman.

John Romberger. Source Medium: Book

John Shoop.

John Shover.

John Stewart. Source Medium: Book

John Swartz. Source Medium: Book

John Weiser Bucher. Source Medium: Book

John Welker. Source Medium: Book

John Werner. Source Medium: Book

John Wert. Source Medium: Book

John William Op Den Graeff. Source Medium: Book

John Witter.

John Wittle.

Johney Stewart.

Jonas Rudy Sr.

Jonas Rudy. Source Medium: Book

Jones household.

Joseph P Leyman.

Joseph Pierce Layman.

Joseph Workman Sr.

Joseph Workman. Source Medium: Book

June Delores Gerrick Pedigree Chart. Source Medium: Book

Jury Family. Source Medium: Book

Kate Wittle.

Katherine Brown. Source Medium: Book

Kathleen (Anna) Shover Stewart. Source Medium: Book

Kathleen A Stewart death certificate. Source Medium: Book

Kathleen A. Stewart (Thomas). Source Medium: Book

Kathleen Romano. Source Medium: Book

Kathleen S Stewart.

Kathleen Stewart. Source Medium: Book

Keefer Book. Source Medium: Book

Keefer family information.

Keefer household. Source Medium: Book

Keefer, Kiefer file. Source Medium: Book

Keeper household. Source Medium: Book

Keifer household. Source Medium: Book

Keiffer household. Source Medium: Book

Kelly family information. Source Medium: Book

Kelly household. Source Medium: Book

Kerstetter Family information.

Kesiah Gaugler. Source Medium: Book

Kieffer family information. Source Medium: Book

Kieffer household. Source Medium: Book

Kile household. Source Medium: Book

Killian Gaugler. Source Medium: Book

Killian household. Source Medium: Book

Kimberline household. Source Medium: Book

Klein hosusehold. Source Medium: Book

Kline household. Source Medium: Book

Knittle household. Source Medium: Book

Kressie Joe Curry.

Kulp family information. Source Medium: Book

Kyle household. Source Medium: Book

Kylian Goukler. Source Medium: Book

Lausman household. Source Medium: Book

Layman household. Source Medium: Book

Layman/Lehman family information.

Laymen household. Source Medium: Book

Laymer family.

Laynon household. Source Medium: Book

Lehman family information. Source Medium: Book

Lehman-Klein marriage record. Source Medium: Book

Lehman-Oberlander marriage. Source Medium: Book

Lehmey household.

Leman household. Source Medium: Book

Lewis G Stewart.

Lewis L Stewart.

Leyman family information. Source Medium: Book

Leyman household. Source Medium: Book

Limmen household. Source Medium: Book

livel.

Liveley family information. Source Medium: Book

Lively household. Source Medium: Book

Livesay family information. Source Medium: Book

Livesey family information. Source Medium: Book

Livezey family information. Source Medium: Book

Livezey household.

Livezley household. Source Medium: Book

Livezly household. Source Medium: Book

Livezly-Culen marriage record. Source Medium: Book

Livezty household.

Livzely household. Source Medium: Book

Loosley household. Source Medium: Book

Lottie Duncan. Source Medium: Book

Lottie V Willard death certificate.

Lottie V. Willard. Source Medium: Book

Louer household. Source Medium: Book

Louis L Stewart burial record. Source Medium: Book

Louis L Stewart. Source Medium: Book

Lucetta Anderson death certificate. Source Medium: Book

Lucetta Anderson. Source Medium: Book

Lucy A Minnick death certificate. Source Medium: Book

Lycoming County PA & Related Families. Source Medium: Book

Lydia B. Thompson. Source Medium: Book

Lydia Mae Thompson.

Lyman household. Source Medium: Book

Lymon household. Source Medium: Book

Lysel household. Source Medium: Book

M.A. Keefer death certificate. Source Medium: Book

Mack Mason death dertificate.

Mack Mason Sr. Source Medium: Book

Mack Mason Sr. death certificate. Source Medium: Book

Mack Mason. Source Medium: Book

Magdalena Bordner.

Magdalene Faver.

Magdalene Trout.

Magdalene Wolffshiel.

Mamie Duncan. Source Medium: Book

Mamie L Duncan.

Mamie Lucetta Duncan death certificate. Source Medium: Book

Mamie Lucetta Duncan. Source Medium: Book

Mamie Luzetta Anderson. Source Medium: Book

Manhattan Hospital. Source Medium: Book

Margaret Bowman.

Margaret Faber. Source Medium: Book

Margaret Kilmartin. Source Medium: Book

Margaret Layman.

Margaret M Keefer death certificate. Source Medium: Book

Margaret M Keefer death record abstract. Source Medium: Book

Margaret M Keefer death record. Source Medium: Book

Margaret M Keefer. Source Medium: Book

Margaret M. Keefer. Source Medium: Book

Margaret Shoop. Source Medium: Book

Margaret Shover death certificate. Source Medium: Book

Margaret T Shover. Source Medium: Book

Maria (Lang) Kieffer. Source Medium: Book

Maria Acri.

Maria Assunta De Stefano.

Maria Brown.

Maria Catharina Werner. Source Medium: Book

Maria Catherine Werner. Source Medium: Book

Maria Elisabetha Bordner. Source Medium: Book

Maria Elisabetha Veltin. Source Medium: Book

Maria Elizabeth Deibler Schup. Source Medium: Book

Maria Elsiabetha Veltin. Source Medium: Book

Maria Kieffer. Source Medium: Book

Maria Magdalena Walter.

Maria Magdelena Walter. Source Medium: Book

Maria Peters.

Maria Sheetz.

Maria Vitale.

Marianna Quintavalle.

Marriage License.

Martha E Stewart death certificate. Source Medium: Book

Martha E Stewart.

Martha Etta Stewart. Source Medium: Book

Martin Apley. Source Medium: Book

Martin Aply.

Martin Connor.

Martin Ebble.

Martin Epley.

Martin Eply.

Martin J O'Connor death certificate. Source Medium: Book

Martin J O'Connor. Source Medium: Book

Martin OConnor. Source Medium: Book

Martin O'Connor. Source Medium: Book

Mary A Guise. Source Medium: Book

Mary Ann O'Connor. Source Medium: Book

Mary Anne Barrett.

Mary C Shannon. Source Medium: Book

Mary E Whittle. Source Medium: Book

Mary Gaugler. Source Medium: Book

Mary Hensel. Source Medium: Book

Mary L Batdorf. Source Medium: Book

Mary Lucetta Anderson. Source Medium: Book

Mary McCabe death certificate. Source Medium: Book

Mary McKim Sheets.

Mary Morrison.

Mary OConnor. Source Medium: Book

Mary O'Connor. Source Medium: Book

Mary Peters death certificate. Source Medium: Book

Mary Piper.

Mary Rowe. Source Medium: Book

Mary Shannon death certificate. Source Medium: Book

Mary Smith. Source Medium: Book

Mary Washington.

Mary Wiittle.

Mary Witter.

Mason household. Source Medium: Book

Mason-Adams.

Mason-Andrews.

Mason-Clayton.

Mason-Cumming.

Mason-Moffett.

Mason-Stephens.

Mason-Thompson marriage.

Mason-Walker.

Mason-Wicker.

Matilda Stewart death record. Source Medium: Book

Maurer household. Source Medium: Book

McCabe household. Source Medium: Book

McCloud household. Source Medium: Book

McCloud-Frye.

McCloud-Keiser.

McKim household.

McKinsey household. Source Medium: Book

McKinsey-Frey.

McKinstry household. Source Medium: Book

McKinstry-McCullough marriage. Source Medium: Book

McLeod household. Source Medium: Book

Melinda Duncan.

Memoranda. Source Medium: Book

Menich household. Source Medium: Book

Menick household. Source Medium: Book

Mertz household. Source Medium: Book

Messerschmidt household. Source Medium: Book

Messerschmidt. Source Medium: Book

Messersmith household. Source Medium: Book

Mich. Leman. Source Medium: Book

Michael A. Keefer. Source Medium: Book

Michael Acri.

Michael Curcio. Source Medium: Book

Michael Garman. Source Medium: Book

Michael Goodman death certificate. Source Medium: Book

Michael Goodman. Source Medium: Book

Michael Gutman. Source Medium: Book

Michael household. Source Medium: Book

Michael Layman. Source Medium: Book

Michael Leyman. Source Medium: Book

Michael Lyman. Source Medium: Book

Michael Oberland. Source Medium: Book

Michael Wittel. Source Medium: Book

Mildred I Michaels death certificate. Source Medium: Book

Mildred Irene Stewart. Source Medium: Book

Mildred Michael.

Mildred Wittle Michaels. Source Medium: Book

Mildred Wittle. Source Medium: Book

Miller family information. Source Medium: Book

Miller Family information.

Miller household. Source Medium: Book

Mini.

Minich household. Source Medium: Book

Minick household. Source Medium: Book

Minick. Source Medium: Book

Mining household.

Minn.

Minnich household. Source Medium: Book

Minnick household. Source Medium: Book

Monn & Related Families. Source Medium: Book

Mons household. Source Medium: Book

Montz household (Mary). Source Medium: Book

Montz household.

Moore household.

More household.

Morrison household. Source Medium: Book

Morrison-Gilmartin.

Mother Faber. Source Medium: Book

Mr. Eddie Mazo.

Mrs Hensel. Source Medium: Book

Mrs Mary Hensel. Source Medium: Book

Mrs Sarah Updegrove death certificate. Source Medium: Book

Mrs. Adeline Wert death certificate. Source Medium: Book

Mrs. Barbara Guise. Source Medium: Book

Mrs. Elizabeth Curry.

Mrs. James McKinsey. Source Medium: Book

Mrs. Thompson. Source Medium: Book

My Family, Dillon, Kelly, Peterson, etc.

My Family-Dillon, Kelly, Peterson, etc. Source Medium: Book

Myrtle A Thompson death certificate. Source Medium: Book

Myrtle A Thompson. Source Medium: Book

Myrtle A. Batdorf birth certificate. Source Medium: Book

Myrtle Thompson. Source Medium: Book

Nail household. Source Medium: Book

Names of Deacons. Source Medium: Book

Neal household.

Neil household.

Neu/Ney/Nye. Source Medium: Book

Nicholas Bittel.

Nicholas Geib.

Nicholas Geip, Sr. Source Medium: Book

Nicholas Gype. Source Medium: Book

Nicholas Mantz (widow Mary).

Nicholas Mantz. Source Medium: Book

Nicholas Montz.

Nicholas Mountz. Source Medium: Book

Nicholas Moutz. Source Medium: Book

Nicolas Geip Jr. Source Medium: Book

Nicolas Gipe. Source Medium: Book

Nina Forsythe.

Nina Washington Forsyth.

Nina Washington Forsythe.

No name Curry.

Oberlander family information. Source Medium: Book

Oberlander household. Source Medium: Book

OConnor household.

O'Connor household. Source Medium: Book

Orsala Marsico. Source Medium: Book

Our Coal Mining Ancestors.

Overland household. Source Medium: Book

Overlander household. Source Medium: Book

Overlander-Baugher marriage.

Overlander-Kipe marriage record. Source Medium: Book

Owen McCabe death certificate. Source Medium: Book

Owen McCabe. Source Medium: Book

PA & Other Assorted Data. Source Medium: Book

PA 1767 Township Tax & Census Lists.

Paolo Romano. Source Medium: Book

Pasquale Barbuscio. Source Medium: Book

Patrick Morrison death certificate. Source Medium: Book

Patrick Morrison.

Pats Family. Source Medium: Book

Paul Romano death certificate. Source Medium: Book

Paul Romano. Source Medium: Book

Pedro Oberlander. Source Medium: Book

Penman family information. Source Medium: Book

Pennman household. Source Medium: Book

Percy C Forsythe.

Percy Campbell Forsythe.

Percy Forsythe.

Peter Baddorf. Source Medium: Book

Peter Batdorf. Source Medium: Book

Peter Botdorf. Source Medium: Book

Peter Braun. Source Medium: Book

Peter Brown. Source Medium: Book

Peter Keefer.

Peter Keffer.

Peter Kiefer. Source Medium: Book

Peter Kieffer Sr.

Peter Kieffer. Source Medium: Book

Peter Klein.

Peter Michael Klein.

Peter Oberlander.

Peter Overlander. Source Medium: Book

Peter Pottorf. Source Medium: Book

Peter Scheffer.

Peter Shaffer.

Peters family information. Source Medium: Book

Peters household. Source Medium: Book

Peters Research.

Phalatien Welcker.

Philip Bordner.

Philip Bortner.

Philip Jacob Bortner.

Philipp Jacob Bortner.

Pietro Guiseppe Romano.

Pietro Romano.

Piper family information.

Piper household. Source Medium: Book

Pnnman household.

Pottierf Jr household. Source Medium: Book

Pottierf, Sr household. Source Medium: Book

Pottorff household.

Pottsville Hospital. Source Medium: Book

Poundstone household. Source Medium: Book

Public Family Tree.

Quland household. Source Medium: Book

Rachel Leyman. Source Medium: Book

Raimondo Barbuscio. Source Medium: Book

Ramberger household. Source Medium: Book

Ramond Burbuish.

Rau/Row. Source Medium: Book

Raymond (Annie) Barbush. Source Medium: Book

Raymond Barbush.

Raymond F Barbush death certificate. Source Medium: Book

Raymond F. Barbush. Source Medium: Book

Raymond Rosario Barbush.

Raymond Rosorio Barbush.

Rebecca Anderson. Source Medium: Book

Rebecca Layman. Source Medium: Book

Rebecca Lehman (Layman) death certificate. Source Medium: Book

Records in Stone II. Source Medium: Book

Reilly household.

Rexroth Family information.

Rieman household.

Robert B Thompson death certificate. Source Medium: Book

Robert B Thompson.

Robert B. Thomspon. Source Medium: Book

Robert C Shover. Source Medium: Book

Robert Charles Shover.

Robert Forsythe.

Robinson household.

Roddy records. Source Medium: Book

Roger Cramer, rogercubs@aol.com. Source Medium: Book

Romano (Romans) household.

Romano family information. Source Medium: Book

Romano household. Source Medium: Book

Romano-McCabe marriage certificate. Source Medium: Book

Romberger All-Family History Site.

Romberger Family information. Source Medium: Book

Romberger Family. Source Medium: Book

Romberger household. Source Medium: Book

Roote household. Source Medium: Book

Rosa Louise Curry.

Rosie household. Source Medium: Book

Rough household. Source Medium: Book

Row household. Source Medium: Book

Rowe family information. Source Medium: Book

Rowe household. Source Medium: Book

Rowe.

Rudy household. Source Medium: Book

Rumberger household. Source Medium: Book

Rutzel Family Genealogy. Source Medium: Book

Rutzel Family. Source Medium: Book

Sallie Duncan.

Sallie Shateen.

Sam Frazier.

Samuel Frazier.

Samuel Peters. Source Medium: Book

Sarah Duncan.

Sarah Elizabeth Faber Wert.

Sarah Elizabeth Wert.

Sarah Mason. Source Medium: Book

Sarah Oberlander.

Sarah Salome Updegrove.

Schamper?/Buffington household. Source Medium: Book

Scheetz household. Source Medium: Book

Schitz family information. Source Medium: Book

Schneck household. Source Medium: Book

Schneider-Cornelius (7/2000). Source Medium: Book

Schnuke household. Source Medium: Book

Schofield Family Tree.

Schupp family information. Source Medium: Book

Sebastian Shover death record abstract. Source Medium: Book

Sebastian Shover. Source Medium: Book

Seibtone household. Source Medium: Book

Selvage & Peterson Families & More. Source Medium: Book

Shadel household. Source Medium: Book

Shaffer family information. Source Medium: Book

Shaffer household. Source Medium: Book

Shaffer Sr household. Source Medium: Book

Shaffer-Swartz marriage record. Source Medium: Book

Shannon household. Source Medium: Book

Shannon-Reath.

Shanon household. Source Medium: Book

Shatteen household.

Shatteen-Hall.

Shattine household.

Shaver household. Source Medium: Book

Sheaffer household. Source Medium: Book

Shearer household.

Sheets household. Source Medium: Book

Sheetz family information. Source Medium: Book

Sheetz household. Source Medium: Book

Shelton household.

Shelton-Freeman marrriage.

Shetz houschold. Source Medium: Book

Shirley Mary Duncan. Source Medium: Book

Shober family information. Source Medium: Book

Shoop family information. Source Medium: Book

Shoop household. Source Medium: Book

Shover household. Source Medium: Book

Shover research.

Shover-Shannon Marriage record. Source Medium: Book

Shovler household.

Shrott. Source Medium: Book

Shup household. Source Medium: Book

Silvia Francesca Barbuscio.

Skelton-Harper marriage.

Smith household. Source Medium: Book

Smith-Reilly marriage.

Snook household. Source Medium: Book

Some of my ancestors. Source Medium: Book

Soop household. Source Medium: Book

Sophia Miller Wirth. Source Medium: Book

Spong-Stewart.

Sproat household. Source Medium: Book

St. Clair household. Source Medium: Book

Stewart family information.

Stewart household. Source Medium: Book

Strayer & Other Families. Source Medium: Book

Stwert (sic) household. Source Medium: Book

Susan McKinsey. Source Medium: Book

Susan McKinsy. Source Medium: Book

Susanna Frantz.

Susanna Franz. Source Medium: Book

Susanna Jury (Schorah). Source Medium: Book

Susanna Rowe. Source Medium: Book

Swartz household. Source Medium: Book

Swoveland household.

Swovler household.

Sylvia Acri. Source Medium: Book

Sylvia F Acri death certificate. Source Medium: Book

Sylvia F Acri. Source Medium: Book

Sylvia F. Acri. Source Medium: Book

Tax lists. Source Medium: Book

Taylor household. Source Medium: Book

Teresa Acri death certificate. Source Medium: Book

Teresa Acri. Source Medium: Book

Teresa Curchi Acri.

Teresa Curcio. Source Medium: Book

The Batdorf Family History, Virgina Faust Batdorf, Mennonite Family History, 1990, Elverson, PA.

The Batdorf Family History.

The Brown (Braun) Family. Source Medium: Book

The Jury Family. Source Medium: Book

The Keefer Family. Source Medium: Book

The Livezey Family. Source Medium: Book

The Lunnys. Source Medium: Book

The Romberger Line. Source Medium: Book

The Rudys of Gods House & Related Families. Source Medium: Book

The Schupp/Shoop Line. Source Medium: Book

The Thomas Liveley Family. Source Medium: Book

Theophilus Forsythe.

Thomas Barrett.

Thomas Batdorf. Source Medium: Book

Thompson family information. Source Medium: Book

Thompson History. Source Medium: Book

Thompson household. Source Medium: Book

Thompson-Batdorf marriage record. Source Medium: Book

Thompson-Hensel Marriage.

Thompson-Key.

Thompson-Mason.

Thompson-Shatteen.

Thomson household.

Tower City Centennial. Source Medium: Book

Traut family information. Source Medium: Book

Trout Family Descendancy. Source Medium: Book

Updagrove household. Source Medium: Book

Updegraf household. Source Medium: Book

Updegrove Family information. Source Medium: Book

Updegrove genealogy. Source Medium: Book

Updegrove household (Updigrove). Source Medium: Book

Updegrove household. Source Medium: Book

Uptegraff Family Genalogy Forum.

Valentin Kne (sic).

Valentin Welcker. Source Medium: Book

Valentine Enders. Source Medium: Book

Valentine Family Tree.

Valentine Neu.

Valentine Ney. Source Medium: Book

Valentine Welcker. Source Medium: Book

Valentine Welker. Source Medium: Book

Veltin-? marriage record. Source Medium: Book

Vencia household. Source Medium: Book

Veronica Kirstetter. Source Medium: Book

Vitale Felice.

Ware/Erdman/Williams/Ingalsbe Family. Source Medium: Book

Warner family information. Source Medium: Book

Warner household. Source Medium: Book

Warner, Beers & Co. Source Medium: Book

Wartzs household. Source Medium: Book

Washington (DC) household.

Washington (Tennia) household.

Washington household.

Weidle household. Source Medium: Book

Weist household. Source Medium: Book

Welcker Data.

Welker family information. Source Medium: Book

Welker Family. Source Medium: Book

Welker household. Source Medium: Book

Welkers in the USA & Nulls from PA. Source Medium: Book

Weller Family Search for Roots. Source Medium: Book

Wendel Traut.

Wendell Trout.

Wendle Trout.

Wenrick household. Source Medium: Book

Wert Family History. Source Medium: Book

Wert family information. Source Medium: Book

Wert Family. Source Medium: Book

Wert household. Source Medium: Book

Wert Sr household. Source Medium: Book

Wert Tree. Source Medium: Book

Wert, Sr. household. Source Medium: Book

Werts (Wertz, Wirtz) Notes. Source Medium: Book

Wertz family information. Source Medium: Book

Wertz household. Source Medium: Book

Wertz Sr household. Source Medium: Book

Whittle household. Source Medium: Book

Widdel household. Source Medium: Book

Wilhelm Minnich. Source Medium: Book

Willard household. Source Medium: Book

William Anderson. Source Medium: Book

William Bager. Source Medium: Book

William Bauger. Source Medium: Book

William Duncan. Source Medium: Book

William Frantz. Source Medium: Book

William Gieseman.

William Giessman. Source Medium: Book

William M. Anderson. Source Medium: Book

William Maurice Anderson.

William Minnich.

William Morris Anderson death certificate. Source Medium: Book

William Morris Anderson. Source Medium: Book

William Row.

William Rowe. Source Medium: Book

William Sheets.

Williamson household. Source Medium: Book

Wirt household. Source Medium: Book

Wirth family information.

Wirth household. Source Medium: Book

Wittel Family Information.

Wittel household. Source Medium: Book

Witter Family Information.

Wittle (Witble) household. Source Medium: Book

Wittle Family information.

Wittle household. Source Medium: Book

Wittle-Minnich marriage record. Source Medium: Book

Witttel household. Source Medium: Book

Wm Baugher. Source Medium: Book

Wm Duncan death certificate. Source Medium: Book

Wm Duncan. Source Medium: Book

Wm Kelly. Source Medium: Book

Wolliam (sic) Baugher. Source Medium: Book

Workman family information. Source Medium: Book

Workman household. Source Medium: Book

Workman. Source Medium: Book

Wurtz/Werts/Wertz Family. Source Medium: Book

Yerigh William Geeseman. Source Medium: Book

Zerber household. Source Medium: Book

About the Author

Marc D. Thompson delved into writing and genealogy at a very early age. He wrote stories, poems, lyrics and family history books. Mr. Thompson went on to write and research in high school and college, earning a BS degree from Moravian College. He has presented genealogical lectures and authored seven family history volumes and recently published "The Fitness Book of Lists" and "Poems...Of Eternal Moments." His other published works appeared in Fighting Chance Magazine, Love's Chance Magazine, Northern Stars Magazine, Offerings, Poetry Motel, Suzerian Enterprises and The Pink Chameleon. He currently pens a monthly health and fitness blog at ideafit.com. Mr. Thompson is a member of the Association of Professional Genealogists and has founded two Genealogy societies. He was the County Coordinator of the Chatham Co, GA USGenweb site and wrote a monthly genealogy column for Atlantic Avenue Magazine. Writing now for over four decades, when he puts pen to paper, eloquent, heat-felt yet real-life truths emerge. Mr. Thompson has been influenced by science, art and believes in what he calls Creatalytical Thinking: The fusion of creativity and analysis to view life more fully.

MARC D. THOMPSON, VIRTUFIT.NET™

www.VirtuFit.net

marc@VirtuFit.net --- Skype: VirtuFit

ideafit: www.ideafit.com/profile/marc-d-thompson

Index of Individuals

?

? (1): 11,84,118
? (10): 25,34,35,80,85,118
? (11): 25,34,35,80,84,118
? (12): 35,42,43,76,85,118
? (13): 35,42,43,76,85,118
? (14): 35,42,43,76,85,118
? (15): 36,43,76,84,118
? (16): 36,43,76,85,118
? (17): 36,43,76,85,118
? (18): 37,43,76,85,118
? (1820): 24,34,69,85
? (19): 37,43,76,85,118
? (2): 20,32,33,69,85,118
? (20): 38,44,76,85,118
? (21): 38,44,76,85,118
? (22): 38,44,76,84,118
? (23): 39,44,45,76,85,118
? (24): 39,44,45,69,84,119
? (25): 42,84,119
? (26): 45,47,48,76,84,119
? (27): 45,47,48,76,85,119
? (28): 84,118
? (29): 84,118
? (3): 20,32,33,69,85,118
? (30): 84,119
? (31): 84,119
? (32): 84,119
? (33): 84,119
? (4): 20,32,33,69,84,118
? (5): 23,33,69,84,118
? (6): 23,33,69,84,118
? (7): 23,33,69,84,118
? (8): 24,34,69,85,118
?, Anna: 39,76,85,119
?, Anne: 30,86,119
?, Flora: 36,76,86
?, Grace: 41,42,86,119
?, Hannah: 13,20,21,22,32,68,69,80,86
?, Hester: 27,36,43,67,69,73,76,79,86
?, Hilda: 14,69,86,119
?, Judy: 42,76,86,119
?, Julia (1): 41,86,119
?, Julia (1910): 86,119
?, Lavinia: 14,70,86
?, Lucretia: 28,38,39,44,67,70,74,76,79,86
?, Lucy: 86,119
?, Lula "Lou": 25,70,86,119
?, Mabel: 86,119

?, Margaret: 16,25,26,28,34,35,65,73,80,86
?, Mary (1820): 28,37,38,39,73,76,79,86
?, Mary (1825): 40,45,46,47,66,76,86
?, May A: 13,21,22,33,68,70,87
?, Minda: 46,76,87,119
?, Minnie: 42,87,119
?, Nancy: 15,23,25,33,68,69,72,74,87
?, Nellie: 29,70,87,119
?, Nora: 41,87,119
?, Rhinor?: 22,33,87,119
?, Stella: 27,80,87,119
?, Tena: 27,35,37,42,76,79,87

A

Adams, Ellen: 21,70,87
Alston, ?: 38,43,44,76,87,119
Alston, Albert: 39,76,87,119
Alston, Benjamin "Ben": 28,38,39,44,67,74,75,76,79,87,119
Alston, Elizabeth "Bessie": 18,28,29,31,38,65,67,68,70,74,75,87,119
Alston, Lucy: 39,76,87
Alston, Mary: 39,76,87
Andrews, Charlotte: 21,87,119

B

Brown, Adam: 32,76,88
Brown, Benjamin: 32,76,88
Brown, Christopher Columbus: 32,76,88
Brown, David?: 39,44,45,76,79,88
Brown, Dorothy Mae: 32,76,88,119
Brown, Elizabeth: 6,11,12,18,19,30,64,66,68,69,73,75,79,88
Brown, Ella Lee: 32,66,76,88,119
Brown, Ellis: 32,76,88
Brown, Eva Mae: 32,75,77,88,119
Brown, George: 13,21,22,68,70,88
Brown, James: 77,88,119
Brown, Joe: 44,47,77,79,88
Brown, Joseph "Joe" (1871): 30,39,40,42,45,66,67,77,88,119
Brown, Joseph "Joe" (1890): 18,30,31,42,64,66,67,68,69,73,75,88,119
Brown, Josephine: 32,77,88
Brown, Lillian "Lillie": 32,77,88,119
Brown, Linton: 40,77,88
Brown, Maria: 70,88
Brown, Mary: 23,70,88
Brown, Rachel: 23,70,88
Brown, Ranie: 6,9,13,14,16,21,68,80,88

Index of Individuals

Brown, Remus: 23,70,89
Brown, Richard: 40,77,89
Brown, Samuel: 23,70,89
Brown, Samuel?: 22,33,89,119
Brown, Simon: 23,70,89
Brown, William: 40,77,89

C

Chapman, Mary: 24,89,120
Clayton, Martha Ann: 15,89
Cumming, Harriet: 22,89,120
Cumming, Henry: 89,120
Curry, Charles "Charlie": 30,70,75,89,120
Curry, Cyrus: 38,77,89
Curry, Delores Ann: 6,7,8,9,11,60,61,68,70,73,75,89
Curry, Duncan C:
18,28,29,31,39,65,67,70,73,74,75,79,89
Curry, Edmonia: 30,70,89
Curry, Elizabeth "Bessie": 29,70,89,120
Curry, Emma: 38,77,89
Curry, Fortune: 28,37,38,39,43,77,79,89
Curry, Frampton: 30,70,90
Curry, Frank: 20,70,90
Curry, Frederick "Fred": 20,70,73,90,120
Curry, Frederick "Freddie":
6,11,12,18,19,31,64,69,73,75,79,90,120
Curry, Gabriel: 77,90
Curry, Hilda: 30,70,90
Curry, Ira: 29,70,90
Curry, Leola: 30,70,90
Curry, Lucretia "Cressie" Jo:
6,8,11,12,13,18,61,65,69,74,75,90,120
Curry, Melvalean: 6,7,60,69,73,74,90
Curry, Nancy: 19,70,90
Curry, Pleasant: 77,90
Curry, Rosa Louise: 29,30,75,90
Curry, Samuel: 20,70,90
Curry, Solomon: 30,70,90,120
Curry, Thomas: 77,90,120
Curry, William: 20,70,90
Curry, William "Willie": 29,70,90,120

D

Dunbar, ?: 77,90
Dunbar, William (1873): 46,77,90,120
Dunbar, William (1898): 77,90
Duncan, Living: 7,9
Dunham, ?: 37,91,120
Durham, ?: 28,91,120

F

Forsythe, Frederick: 26,80,91
Forsythe, Hattie: 26,80,91
Forsythe, Mildred: 18,72,91,120
Forsythe, Nelson: 25,34,35,74,91
Forsythe, Nina: 17,18,70,80,91
Forsythe, Percy Campbell:
6,11,16,17,19,28,65,66,68,72,73,75,80,81,91
Forsythe, Robert J Washington:
6,8,11,13,19,61,64,68,75,79,80,91
Forsythe, Theodore: 27,80,91,120
Forsythe, Theodore (Theopolis):
16,25,26,28,35,64,66,67,73,75,80,81,91,120
Frazier, "Lillie": 91,120
Frazier, "Mamie": 42,77,91,120
Frazier, "Sadie" B: 91,120
Frazier, ?: 45,47,48,77,91,120
Frazier, Andrew: 91
Frazier, Arthur: 91
Frazier, Benjamin "Ben": 46,77,92,120
Frazier, Benjamin (1889): 41,42,77,91,120
Frazier, Benjamin (1904): 91
Frazier, Bernice: 92
Frazier, Betty: 46,77,92
Frazier, Butler (1898): 77,92,120
Frazier, Butler (1925): 92
Frazier, Clinton King: 92
Frazier, Darthean: 92
Frazier, Eliza: 92
Frazier, Eria: 92
Frazier, Garling: 92
Frazier, Helen: 42,77,92
Frazier, Henry: 77,92,120
Frazier, James E: 92
Frazier, James N: 92
Frazier, John W: 42,77,92
Frazier, Josephine "Josie": 46,77,92,120
Frazier, Laura: 92
Frazier, Lee G: 93
Frazier, Mary: 46,77,93
Frazier, Minnie: 41,77,93,120
Frazier, Nancy (1865): 46,77,93
Frazier, Nancy (1889): 18,30,31,40,66,67,68,69,75,93
Frazier, Robert: 41,77,93,120
Frazier, Rose: 93
Frazier, Samuel "Sam":
30,40,41,47,65,66,67,68,73,93,120
Frazier, Samuel (1882): 41,77,93
Frazier, Samuel (1918): 93
Frazier, Sidney: 46,77,93
Frazier, Smart: 40,45,47,48,66,67,77,79,93

Index of Individuals

Frazier, Susan (1881): 46,77,93
Frazier, Susan (1902): 42,77,93
Frazier, Taylor: 46,77,93,120
Frazier, Tenor: 46,78,93
Frazier, Virginia: 93
Frazier, William: 94
Frazier, William "Willie" (1898): 94,120
Frazier, William "Willie" (1898): 42,78,94,120
Frazier, William "Willie" King: 94,120

G

Gillison, "Tillie": 94,120
Gillison, ?: 41,94,120
Glover?, Lina: 30,39,40,42,44,66,67,78,94
Gould, ?: 32,94,120
Grant, ?: 32,94,120
Green, ?: 11,94,120

H

Hall, Susan: 25,94,121
Hapton, Elizabeth: 25,34,35,81,94
Harris, ?: 11,94,121
Harris, Carrie L: 94
Harris, Sallie: 94
Hay?, Martha: 46,94,121
Hay?, Millie?: 39,44,45,47,78,79,94
Howard, ?: 18,94,121

J

Jones, ?: 45,47,48,78,94,121
Jones, Minda: 40,45,47,66,67,78,95

K

Key, Mary: 24,95,121

M

Mason, "Maggie": 70,95,121
Mason, "Mattie" May: 95,121
Mason, Addie: 70,95
Mason, Aggie: 14,73,80,95,121
Mason, Alfred (1825): 13,20,21,22,33,68,70,80,95
Mason, Alfred (1868): 22,70,95
Mason, Alonzo: 15,70,95
Mason, Andrew: 21,70,95
Mason, Anne: 95
Mason, Anne "Annie": 70,95,121
Mason, Anne Lee: 11,71,95,121
Mason, Austin: 14,71,95
Mason, Benjamin: 71,95
Mason, Bessie: 71,95
Mason, Cleveland: 22,71,95
Mason, Cute: 95

Mason, Daniel: 71,95
Mason, Dicey: 14,71,96
Mason, Eddie: 71,96
Mason, Edward "Ned": 6,9,13,14,16,22,65,69,80,96,121
Mason, Ella: 15,71,96
Mason, Flander A: 24,96,121
Mason, Freeman: 96
Mason, George (1861): 21,71,96
Mason, George (1926): 11,71,96
Mason, George W: 14,71,96,121
Mason, Jacob "Jake": 21,71,96,121
Mason, James (1872): 14,71,96
Mason, James (1884): 96
Mason, James?: 21,71,96
Mason, Jane: 14,71,96
Mason, Janice: 15,71,96
Mason, Jefferson D: 21,71,96
Mason, Jesse: 10,11,71,96
Mason, John: 96
Mason, John Dooly: 11,71,96
Mason, Josephine: 21,22,71,96,121
Mason, Linda: 21,71,96
Mason, Living: 96
Mason, Mack (1880): 6,7,9,10,13,16,19,64,65,67,68,69,73,74,75,80,81,97
Mason, Mack (1914): 11,71,97
Mason, Maria: 11,71,97
Mason, Martha L: 97
Mason, Melvin: 11,80,97
Mason, Mollie: 71,97
Mason, Moses?: 20,32,33,71,97,121
Mason, Noah (1848): 21,71,97
Mason, Noah (1895): 97
Mason, Oliver: 15,71,97
Mason, Omar: 97
Mason, Plum: 14,71,97
Mason, Reuben: 71,97
Mason, Robert B: 11,71,97
Mason, Thomas (1853): 21,71,97
Mason, Thomas (1880): 71,97
Mason, Viola: 97
Mason, Willard: 71,97
Mason, Willie (1890): 97
Mason, Willie (1899): 97
Mason, Willis: 71,98
Mazo, Cellina: 98
Mazo, D "Gobby": 98,121
Mazo, Living (1): 9,98,121

Index of Individuals

Mazo, Living (1954): 11,98,121
Mazo, Living (1956): 98
Mazo, Living (1958): 98,121
Mazo, Living (1959): 98
Mazo, Living (1961): 98
Mazo, Living (1962): 98
Mazo, Living (1970): 98
Mazo, Living (3): 98,121
Mazo, Living (4): 98,121
Mazo, Living (5): 98,121
Mazo, M (1963): 98
Mazo, M (1967): 98
Mazo, Ned "Eddie":
6,7,9,11,13,19,60,61,65,66,67,71,73,75,80,98,121
Middleton, Daniel: 21,71,98
Middleton, Dicey: 98
Middleton, Mary: 98
Miller, ?: 32,98,121
Moffett, Carrie: 21,98,121
Morgan, Sallie: 15,23,24,25,34,65,68,69,71,73,74,75,98
Morgan, Thomas: 24,34,68,72,99

P

Palmer, William?: 14,99,121

R

Reeves?, King: 21,22,99,121
Robinson, ?: 36,43,78,99,121
Robinson, Anna: 37,78,99
Robinson, Dolly: 37,78,99
Robinson, Elizabeth: 36,37,78,99
Robinson, Emma: 36,78,99
Robinson, John: 37,78,99
Robinson, Joseph: 36,78,99
Robinson, Mary: 16,26,27,28,36,64,65,67,73,76,99
Robinson, Robert: 27,36,43,67,69,73,78,79,99
Robinson, Thomas J: 72,99
Robinson, Willis: 37,78,99

S

Shateen, ?: 24,34,72,99,121
Shatteen, Anne: 6,9,15,16,23,68,72,80,99
Shatteen, Beatrice: 99
Shatteen, Carrie: 99
Shatteen, Frank: 100
Shatteen, Isaac: 34,72,100
Shatteen, James: 25,72,100,121
Shatteen, Jesse: 34,72,100
Shatteen, Jessie: 100
Shatteen, Lillie: 25,72,100
Shatteen, Linnie: 25,72,100

Shatteen, Linnie Ann: 100
Shatteen, Mary "Mamie": 100,121
Shatteen, Mary Jane: 100
Shatteen, Mason: 15,23,24,25,34,68,72,100
Shatteen, Nathan: 100
Shatteen, Rena: 100
Shatteen, Virgil: 34,100
Shatteen, Zebedee: 100
Stephens, Mary Ellen: 100,121

T

Thompson, " Abbie": 72,100,121
Thompson, Adam: 40,45,46,47,66,78,100
Thompson, Catherine: 47,78,101
Thompson, Cato C: 24,72,101
Thompson, Cornelius: 24,72,101
Thompson, Daniel?: 78,101
Thompson, Ellen: 47,78,101
Thompson, Eva: 30,40,41,45,64,66,67,73,74,101
Thompson, George: 47,78,101
Thompson, Henry: 24,72,101
Thompson, J J: 24,72,101
Thompson, Joshua A: 24,72,101,121
Thompson, Julia: 24,72,101
Thompson, Larfield: 72,101
Thompson, Layer: 24,72,101
Thompson, Living (1): 7,9,60,69,73,74,101,121
Thompson, Living (1935): 7,9
Thompson, Living (2004): 75,101
Thompson, Lornie: 72,101
Thompson, Maria: 47,78,101
Thompson, Peter: 6,9,15,16,25,68,72,73,80,101
Thompson, Samuel?: 23,33,72,101,121
Thompson, Sarah "Sallie" A Shalteen:
6,7,9,10,13,15,19,64,66,68,69,74,80,102,121
Thompson, Seymour: 23,24,72,102
Thompson, Stephen (1820):
15,23,25,33,68,69,72,78,102
Thompson, Stephen (1879): 24,72,102
Thompson, Susan: 72,102
Thompson, Thomas: 47,78,102
Thompson, Thomas?: 78,102

W

Walker, Ellen: 21,102
Walker, Pheobe: 21,72,102
Washington, ? (1): 35,42,43,78,102,122
Washington, ? (1910): 78,102
Washington, Aaron: 35,78,102
Washington, Albert Ernest Robinson: 28,78,102

Index of Individuals

Washington, Benjamin?: 42,102

Washington, Charles H Robinson: 28,72,102

Washington, D C: 42,78,102,122

Washington, Daniel?: 42,102

Washington, Dara: 78,103

Washington, Elizabeth "Betsy": 35,78,103,122

Washington, Essie: 78,103

Washington, George: 78,103

Washington, Harold: 78,80,103

Washington, Hasilar Neter: 78,103

Washington, Joseph: 78,103

Washington, Joseph "Joe" (1835):
27,35,37,43,78,79,103,122

Washington, Joseph "Joe" (1868):
16,26,27,28,37,67,68,72,78,79,103,122

Washington, Lottie: 79,103

Washington, Nina:
6,11,16,17,19,26,64,65,68,72,73,76,79,103

Washington, Rose: 79,103

Washington, Samuel: 79,103

Washington, Smart: 35,36,79,103

Washington, Solomon: 79,103

Washington, Susan: 79,103

Washington, William: 36,79,103

Washington, William "Billie": 79,104,122

Wicker, Leila: 14,104,122

Williams, Emery Ardel: 75,104,122

Williams, Living (1): 13,104,122

Williams, Living (10): 104,122

Williams, Living (11): 104,122

Williams, Living (12): 104,122

Williams, Living (13): 104,122

Williams, Living (14): 104,122

Williams, Living (2): 75,104,122

Williams, Living (3): 75,104,122

Williams, Living (4): 75,104,122

Williams, Living (5): 75,104,122

Williams, Living (6): 75,104,122

Williams, Living (7): 75,104,122

Williams, Living (8): 75,104,122

Williams, Living (9): 104,122

www.ingramcontent.com/pod-product-compliance
Lightning Source LLC
Chambersburg PA
CBHW081152270326
41930CB00014B/3118